WHEN I WAS YOUR AGE

WHEN I WAS YOUR AGE

IRELAND'S GRANDPARENTS SHARE MEMORIES & WISDOM

Valerie Cox

HACHETTE
BOOKS
IRELAND

First published in Ireland in 2022 by
HACHETTE BOOKS IRELAND

A CIP catalogue record for this book is available from the British Library.

ISBN 978 1 39971 227 9

Typeset in Bembo Book Std
Printed and bound in Great Britain by Clays Ltd, Elcograf, S.p.A

Hachette Books Ireland policy is to use papers that are natural, renewable
and recyclable products and made from wood grown in sustainable forests.
The logging and manufacturing processes are expected to conform to the
environmental regulations of the country of origin.

Hachette Books Ireland
8 Castlecourt Centre
Castleknock
Dublin 15, Ireland

A division of Hachette UK Ltd
Carmelite House, 50 Victoria Embankment, EC4Y 0DZ

www.hachettebooksireland.ie

Contents

For my own grandparents,
William and Ellen Tucker and Terence and May FitzPatrick.
Precious memories.

Dear Reader

Becoming a grandparent is a precious moment in people's lives, one that gives rise to many emotions – from joy to trepidation to a keen protective instinct – as we're enveloped in a new kind of love. It can also lead to fresh consideration of our own early lives. Speaking from experience, the birth of a new generation in our family opened up a well of memories from my younger life, as I thought about how times had changed, and what that might mean in the lives of my grandchildren.

Of course, it's not black and white – so many things about life today for children are better: education, career opportunities, acceptance of difference and societal tolerance in general.

But perhaps other things have been lost. There is no doubt that life when I was a child was simpler. Choices were fewer, as were life expectations. The world seemed like a smaller place and access to information was more limited, something that has both its advantages and drawbacks. Children now have a much wider range of influence in their lives, partly through technology and social media, and perhaps there is something to be gained from recognising the value of a time when the life of a child was more contained, its pleasures less dependent on material things.

The interviews featured within these pages capture the changing fabric of society across three generations, from how childhood was for Ireland's grandparents, to their view of what has changed today – for better or worse – and what wisdom they would like to pass along. Consistently, we see shared wonder at the advent of grandparenthood – a cherished rite of passage that carries all of the love but less of the pressure of parenthood. The pieces describe beautifully that bond and how grand-parenthood often offers people a chance to do it again, only better!

While there is concern for the future of the upcoming generation, there is also great hope, and faith in young people to navigate the special challenges of this era, and find creative and sustaining solutions.

The pieces also reflect the values that people

hold dear – the true wealth that comes from love, compassion and kindness, over the world of material things, and the life values that the older generation wish to pass on.

It was a pleasure to interview the remarkable subjects for this book – some well-known names, others simply individuals with interesting perspectives and stories, from across the broad spectrum of Irish society. I hope you enjoy reading this snapshot of social history as much as I've enjoyed bringing it together. And that it gives you a chance to consider, young or old, the values you hold dear, the memories you'd like to pass along, and those things in life that are most important to you.

Lots of love
Valerie Cox
September 2022

Grandchildren from age eleven to six:
Brian, Henry, Ellie & Michael

A Cheque from the President
... and from Guinness

MARY KENNEDY

Broadcaster, author and grandmother Mary Kennedy grew up in the Dublin suburb of Clondalkin, after her parents moved out from the city having been reared around the cattle markets of the North Circular Road. Her mother and her mother's sister Eilish had a double wedding, and then the two sisters bought homes side by side. 'I consider myself one of seven, not four,' says Mary, having had three boy cousins right next door.

This large extended family even had two televisions. 'Before it was fashionable, because there was one in our house and one next door, and on a Saturday night we were divided along gender lines

– the two men and the boys would be in one house watching *Match of the Day*, and my mother and Auntie Eilish and the girls in the other house watching Gay Byrne on *The Late Late Show*.'

The families spent holidays and Christmases together, alternating one year to the next for the seasonal dinner. 'It was a very normal upbringing, we didn't have anything to spare, moneywise. My mother, who had worked in the civil service, was subject to the marriage bar when she got married. But even if she hadn't been, she would have resigned her job. She felt once she got married, her place was in the home as a mother and a homemaker, and she absolutely loved it.'

> My mother would put the porridge on
> before she left for mass each morning.

Mary, who is sixty-eight this year, is the eldest of four children and says her earliest memories are dictated by pictures in photo albums. 'I really feel that is how I remember things – visitors coming, trips to the zoo for communion and birthdays. I recall starting school with my cousin William, who was three months younger than me. If you got into trouble in school in those days, you would not mention it at home, or you'd get into far more serious trouble!'

Theirs was a simple life, punctuated by religion and homemaking. 'My mother and Uncle Tom next door would go to half seven mass every morning, and she would put the porridge on before she left. She would also switch on the electric heater in the bathroom. She would have the fire on downstairs as well.'

The family always sat down for tea. 'I remember Mam used to ration the butter because my brother John *loved* butter and there would be none left by the end of the week, and we didn't have the money to be buying extra. She had little Tupperware containers, and everybody was given their butter ration for the week and you would do with it what you liked. John was always bartering once he ran out!'

As they were growing up, Mary, her siblings and her cousins had a very close relationship with their grandmother, Annie Dowdall from Newtown in Carlow. 'She came to Dublin in 1911 to get married. The family had no money for education beyond primary school, but Annie was very bright, so the teachers kept her on as a helper. She always had this expression if we did well in a test or anything – "The sod of turf wasn't wasted on you" – because in her time every child brought in a sod of turf for the fire. In my school memories, the heat was put on for a couple of hours in the morning and then it was turned off and no matter how cold it got, you just got on with it!'

The family had no money for education beyond primary school, but Annie was very bright, so the teachers kept her on as a helper.

Annie visited regularly. 'My mother and her sisters were very devoted to their mother, who lived until she was 102.' Although in later years she was less mobile, she remained 'sharp as a tack. She got the cheque from the president, and a much more generous cheque from Guinness, where her husband had worked; she was a Guinness widow. We used to always have a thing on Friday – who was going to go and get Granny's tablets? You'd go to the pharmacy in James's Gate and pick them up.'

Mary recalls family holidays, which her adored gran always joined them on. Her mother and

Auntie Eilish would look up the ads in the back of the *Independent* in January, and come summer they would set off for places like Skerries, borrowing a car to get there and staying for a month. The two dads came on holiday to Skerries for the month but, for the second fortnight, they went to work into Dublin city on the train every day, returning in the evening.

'One year we decided to go a bit further, and we got a house in Geesala in Mayo. We had cars by then and it took two days to get there. We stopped by Lough Owel in Mullingar for a picnic, and then we overnighted in Elphin, in a bed and breakfast, and continued on the next morning.

'We arrived at teatime, and it was a big house. It's a hotel now but in those days it was a house for rent, and it was also the medical centre. I remember we arrived on a Sunday night, and on the Monday morning I pulled back the curtains to see men's backs all along the windowsill, waiting to go in to see the district nurse!

'We absolutely loved that house. It had a huge kitchen, but at high tide there was a stream that ran through the room! We loved jumping from the kitchen table to the sink, it was great fun. Another year we went to Spiddal. It was 1969, and I remember the two dads watching the Battle of the Bogside coverage that year on TV. I have two brothers and three male cousins, and they were absolutely wild. I can remember one of the beds coming through the ceiling into the living room because they were jumping up and down!'

After her Leaving Certificate Mary got a scholarship to UCD. 'There was absolutely no way I would have been able to otherwise. I studied six hours a night for the Leaving Cert, went to UCD, studied arts and then went back to my alma mater to teach! After I did my diploma, I went to Brittany for a year to university on an exchange to teach English. It was lovely, to live the French life. When I was there, my father had a heart attack and died, he was fifty-nine. He died on the golf course. I had intended to do a second year in Brittany, but I came back because the salary was needed and I got a job in my local school.

'At the same time, I saw an ad in the paper looking for part-time continuity announcers in RTÉ, so I applied and told nobody. After all, I was from Clondalkin, and that would be getting ideas above your station! I never thought I'd get it, but I did.

'My mother was very shy, and very nervous, and I think she felt that I might lose the run of myself. My father, on the other hand, who had died in March of the previous year, would have *loved* it. He was a big performer, he was in the Clondalkin Dramatic Society, and he would have dined out on the fact that I was working in RTÉ!'

Mary went on to have a stellar career with the national broadcaster, a high point being presenting the Eurovision Song Contest in 1995, and her many years co-presenting the much-loved *Nationwide*. She is the author of six books, including her memoir *Paper Tigers* and her most recent book *Journey to the Well*, co-written with her sister Deirdre Ní Chinnéide.

Mary has four grown children and her first grandchild, Paddy, was born in 2019. Her daughter Eva is now expecting baby number three. Paddy's birth brought back memories of her own mother, all she did for Mary when her own children were small, and that special bond she had with the grandchildren. 'She was their childminder when I was teaching. She did everything for me, even though she thought I should be at home. They absolutely *adored* her, all of them, and they loved the sleepovers in her house. That was nice for her too as she was a widow.

'I remember when Paddy was born, a sense of it being so surreal to have the next generation. With tiny new babies, it takes you unawares, that feeling of "This is my tribe", the continuation of the family line. I met him the day he was born. Eva phoned to say he was born at seven in the morning, and I think I was in Limerick by eleven!

'There are stages in life for everything, and this is *my* moment to have that combination of working part-time and being a grandmother. I would hate to be working so much that I couldn't see my grandchildren. Covid has been abysmal, we have missed so much. Paddy had his first birthday down in Limerick, it was hard. I remember at Christmas in lockdown, I made up a little hamper and drove down to Limerick very early in the morning, and I left it on the porch and got back into my car, and stayed in the driveway. When Paddy came out to the car, he couldn't understand – "Nana, you not coming in?" It was heartbreaking!

'He is three now and he has a little sister Holly, who is eighteen months, she is just adorable. The lovely thing about modern life is the smartphone and all the videos; even if you don't see them every day you can have a relationship over FaceTime. For grandparents who have family abroad, it is a lifeline.

'I am delighted by the way that Eva is so into maintaining traditions that she knew as a child. Reading *The Night Before Christmas* last thing on

Christmas Eve, and the eldest child bringing the candle in to the front room. She does all of those things. I did them as a kid, we did them when they were kids, and now she is doing them again with her kids.

'They were on holidays in the rain for two weeks in Kilkee. She bought the buckets and spades, and sent a photograph of little Holly standing outside a shop, probably a pound shop, just looking in at all the plastic toys, and Eva said, "This could have been me!"'

Mary has very specific wishes for her grandchildren. 'I want them to relish their youth and not to be caught up in study, as I was. I put my life on hold for many, many years. I remember being holed up in the back bedroom and all the other kids out playing rounders on the street. I was so belt and braces. Most children would say, "We don't have to do that poet, he came up last year," but I would do him anyway *just* in case.

> They were on holidays in the rain
> for two weeks in Kilkee. She bought
> the buckets and spades, and sent a
> photograph of little Holly standing
> outside a shop, probably a pound shop,
> just looking in at all the plastic toys.

'I would also like my grandchildren to realise that success is measured in the way that you relate to people, the relationships that you have, and the relationships that you nurture. For a lot of people success is measured in wealth and status. I would really like my grandchildren to feel that those are not important things. As long as you have a roof over your head, that you are happy, that those around you are happy, that you can have treats, and sustain your family and friends and enjoy life – that is what is important. As Gay Byrne said, the graveyard is full of people who thought they were indispensable.

'I would like my grandchildren to have the mentality that it is not about being the biggest and the best, but more about being fulfilled. I would like them to be community and relationship focused.'

For Mary, being a grandmother is something to treasure. 'It is not given to everybody, but it is an absolute gift and a joy. The stage that Paddy and Holly are at now – they are funny, they are innocent, they are beautiful human beings. They are just full of wonder and excitement at everything. My children obviously had all of those attributes, but I don't think I relished them in the same way that I do now. I am older now and I was working much more back then, and racing and chasing.

'When my own children were small I would make the tea, and if the four of them were sitting around and laughing and joking with each other, I would say, "Okay, they are fine, I will go out now and put on a wash." Whereas now I would say, "Forget the wash, do it later, sit down and enjoy your children."'

Grandchildren from age three to twenty months:
Paddy & Holly

The Last of the Tenements

PEIG MCMANUS

Dubliner Peig McManus grew up in the last of the city's tenements, on North King Street in Dublin 7. 'There was one room, with a lean-to off it, where there would be the cot. There was a fireplace and a chest of drawers. We had a wardrobe, a table with two chairs and a bed. There was a bucket in the room as well, as there were no inside toilets.

'In our house, there were about six families who all had children. There was a lady who lived at the top of the house, she was blind, and everybody gave her dinner and minded her. There was one couple who had no children, which was a major thing to us. On the landing, there was a sink where people could wash their clothes. On the ground floor, there was a shop that my granny ran with my aunt. It was a newsagent and tobacco shop, and they sold turf during the war. My aunt used to keep cats, and I remember a man would come into the shop and say, "A stone of coal please, and no cat shite."'

These are the childhood memories of eighty-three-year-old Peig, daughter of Christopher Dowdall and Bridie Malone. 'I have two sisters and three brothers alive, but I also had a brother, Christopher, and a sister, Anne, who both died. It was a big family, but not as big as it could have been; back then it wasn't unusual for women to have ten or twelve children.

'My mother was married when she was nineteen. My earliest memories of my mammy were when she was very sick, she had TB for her whole lifetime. She used to sing all the time, "Pack up your troubles in your old kit bag", and she made bread every day.

> There was one room, with a lean-to off it,
> where there would be the cot. There was a
> fireplace and a chest of drawers. We had a
> wardrobe, a table with two chairs and a bed.

'We had no space in the tenements, but it was a lovely community. I hope I am not romanticising it, because obviously there were upsets with people living so close to each other, but my memory of it was that people really cared for one another. They would give you a loan of sugar, or milk, they shared what little they had. They were kind and looked after all the kids.

'The road outside was a busy one with horses and carts and bicycles. When I was very young I remember Mammy bringing us up to what they called "the temple" – it was a park near the Law Society, and we played there. We moved out to Cabra then. Ireland was a young country at the time, in the shadow of a war, and they managed to do a huge clearance of the slums, the tenements. They built new houses, in Cabra West, where we went to, and Drimnagh, Ballyfermot, Whitehall, lots of places on the outskirts of the city. I was five when we moved. It would have been 1944.

'And, oh, the difference! For the first time we had a flush toilet, a bath, bedrooms to ourselves, a front and back garden, even a letterbox! That was massive. I remember my mam saying, "Oh, we have our own letterbox!" And then later saying, "I never knew what misery it would bring, all the bills coming through it."

'The day we moved out to Cabra, there were all

these yellow flowers in the garden. Daddy said they were dandelions, so we ran out and picked them all, and put them through the letterbox!

'My dad was a brush maker, but his passion – and his downfall – was that he was a bookie. And a gambler. We all knew each other in the tenements, but when we moved out to Cabra, no one knew each other. I remember my father saying, "Don't make friends with these people, they will want to live in your ear!" And he always said that we would only be there until we found something better. But when we got to Cabra – the freedom! We would play skipping rope and sing songs, play ring-a-ring-a-rosie ... We played rounders; doctors and nurses; catch a girl, kiss a girl ... We learned all sorts of skills, really.

People really cared for one another.
They would give you a loan of sugar, or milk, they shared what little they had. They were kind and looked after all the kids.

'We lived on Broombridge Road and we were blessed because over the bridge was the canal and we could swim across the canal. A man called Mr Waldron used to supervise, and he would say,

"Jump!" and we would jump in and doggy-paddle. We had such freedom. We learned how to negotiate dangers. We had to walk to school, and cross roads. I feel that children are so deprived of freedom now.

'I went to King's Inns Street school. Mam used to let me out on the street to go to school, which was about five hundred yards up the road, and when I would get up to the corner, there was a woman who had a vegetable shop, and she would see me and take me into the school.

'When we went out to Cabra West, we went to our new school, my sister Bridie and me. It was a convent, and Mammy left us there and we were devastated. We didn't want to be there! We were afraid of the big building, you know?

'Because we were from the tenements, we were like snotty-nosed little urchins. One of the little kids said, "Please, miss, can I go to the lav?", and the nun said, "You *can*, but you *may* not," and the little one wet herself. That was the first time I realised that other people spoke differently, and people from different classes were treated differently.

'I had two wonderful teachers, Ms Moriarty and Ms McCarthy. Ms McCarthy was from Kerry, and she taught me a love of English. I was a curious child, but I missed a lot of school because my mam was so sick. Mam went into hospital when I was seven and when I was ten, and I always thought she was going to die. It was terrifying. That wasn't just our experience though, that was very common back then. A lot of people had tuberculosis.

'I left school at fourteen. Myself and my friend got a job in a hat factory first, but then I got a job in a brush factory. My husband worked in the post office. I'd met him at a dance in Mills Hall, which was beside the Shelbourne hotel. It was a kind of a jazz club. I was twenty-one when I met Paddy.

Peig and Paddy got married on St Stephen's Day. 'I didn't like the whole big wedding thing, I got a loan of a beautiful dress. It was lashing rain the whole day, a sign of things to come! We put a deposit on a house, which was a massive thing. It was a house in Marino. Paddy and I both wanted to move to that area, because it was absolutely gorgeous, a very old neighbourhood. But the house was a complete shell. We had a very interesting time!

'Leaving my own home was not easy, so I would get two buses into town and visit my mam, and then home to make Paddy his dinner. But when my daughter Breda started school, I met lots of other mothers and it was fantastic. We set up a little committee, and we would have community games and all that, it was just marvellous. My kids would play, I used to tie the gate, and there would be about ten kids in the garden.'

Peig had five children, three girls and two boys, but her first was born before she was married and, as was often the case in those days, was adopted. 'Years later I wanted to find her so I got in touch with the original adoption society and they put me in touch with Marie when I was about fifty. I was so relieved to get in touch with her. It had been a bone of contention. I had told my husband, but nobody else knew. It was like a dark secret that I lived with for so long. But Paddy wrote to Marie, and sent her a beautiful Tara brooch. She is very much a part of our family now, we speak every Sunday. She is the image of me. You talk about nature and nurture – I never raised her, but she has such strong traits of mine.'

We had poverty, but we didn't have poverty
of spirit. We had freedom, and we could go
out and run around and kiss boys!

Peig has a special bond with all of her grand-children. 'I had eleven grandchildren but one of my grandsons died so I have ten alive now, ranging from twenty-six to fifteen.

'When I first saw the eldest, Holly, it was so emotional. Absolutely. Something you can't describe. It was a miracle, that's all I can think of. I want my grandchildren to have a life where they can live in harmony with themselves and each other. I hope they find a passion in life, to do things that they love.

'I think life is much harder for my grandchildren. We had poverty, but we didn't have poverty of spirit. We had freedom, and we could go out and run around and kiss boys! That was our big thing. I wanted to fall in love and be in love and get married and live happily ever after. We didn't have many other aspirations.

'People think that you were deprived if you were out working at fourteen – but I called that the university of life! You were making a contribution to your family, you were helping. You had to manage your money. You had to go into work and learn a skill and learn how to get on with people. It was a whole different type of university.'

Peig grew up at a time when the church was very influential in Ireland. 'I was quite religious as a child, I wanted to be a nun. Everything was a mortal sin. Going to confession, it instilled in you a sense of shame and guilt. From a very young age I was always trying to be good, but I never made it! The whole notion of confession, confessing a sin … you didn't even know what a sin was! Stumbling into the confession box and telling a priest you were disobedient and didn't do what your mother told you.

'But I have a belief in God deeply ingrained in me. I know there is something more than this life. I probably got that from my father, who was raised by the Christian Brothers, but wasn't religious. I loved the Exposition of the Blessed Sacrament. The incense and the Latin hymns, and the miraculous medal, I loved all the ceremony. I liked that part of the church.

'I was very lucky that at the time I was having children, there was a revolution in women's rights. Contraception revolutionised women's lives, you didn't have to have ten children anymore.

'I got to go out to work as well, and earn my own money, but I liked being at home for the children too. Nowadays, women who have a mortgage and all, they have no choice but to juggle three jobs and childcare. I was able to mind my mother back then as well, because I wasn't always working outside the home. But nowadays people have to get home care, because the women are missing.'

In years to come, Peig would like her grandchildren to remember her 'as someone who loved them very much. They all think I'm mad, I'm a mad granny. I used to let them dance in the puddles, and in the rain, and climb Bray Head. I want them to remember me as a mad granny!'

Grandchildren from age twenty-six to sixteen:
Holly, Clea, Niamh, Paris, Tomás, Jasmine,
Joseph (RIP), Hermes, Colum, Anna & Matthew

Making Hideouts and Climbing Trees

BERTIE AHERN

An idyllic childhood spent in a rural oasis in urban Dublin are former taoiseach Bertie Ahern's memories of growing up in the 1950s. 'My father, Con, worked in All Hallows College, a seminary for the Vincentian order. We were allowed play in the grounds, so we had a great time. They had fantastic sporting facilities. We played on the farm there and helped my dad. As kids we did a bit of everything, fed the pigs, milked the cows, fed the cows, collected the cows to bring them in. I would have started helping my dad from about four years old, mixing buckets of meal and mashing turnips and all that.'

Bertie, who is seventy-one years old this year, was born and reared in Drumcondra, the youngest of six children to his parents Con and Julia, five of whom survive. 'We had a brother who died when he was a baby, John Joseph. We never forget him.'

Because he and his siblings had plenty of space to run wild, they were always on the go. 'We would make hideouts, dens, climb trees, there were trees everywhere in All Hallows. We would come home from school, go to the college and be there until dark. We'd help my dad with the odd job here and there, and as we got older, we would do bigger jobs, particularly on the weekend.'

> We played on the farm there and helped my dad. As kids we did a bit of everything, fed the pigs, milked the cows, fed the cows, collected the cows to bring them in.

He recalls that food was the main payment back then, until summer holidays in secondary school, when he made his first earnings. Sporting memories are of regular matches with his father supporting St Pat's student team. 'Life always struck me as very simple in those days. We had a charmed time, being in the college. Every week I would go to a St Pat's club match with my dad. The students' college then had a side called Éireann's Hope. Dad knew a lot of them.

'The guys my dad worked with were all from north County Dublin, mainly from St Margaret's, and they were all involved in St Margaret's Football Club so we used to go to those matches too. They were great days. There was a lot of talk recently about a fight in Croke Park [an on-field fracas between players and officials] but when I was going to those matches there was a fight every week! Nobody worried about the fights then!'

Autumn was a favourite time of year, and the harvest. 'My mother would make apple tarts, we all loved them. Nobody has ever made an apple tart like my mother. All those simple things – I was brought up on everything being baked. My mother baked for Ireland – brown bread, soda bread, apple pies. All those simple things in life. That's what I want for my grandkids.

'We have a family allotment, and I have it divided into the names of my grandkids. It's in the estuary in Malahide. I was determined that my grandchildren would not think that food grew on supermarket shelves, already wrapped! I wanted them to learn about growing things, and the seasons, and when to plant and all that.

'I have a go at growing everything. Because they are kids, I'm trying to show variety. So we have cabbage, potatoes, lettuce, onions, scallions … And we have a tunnel, where we grow tomatoes and grapes.'

Bertie has six grandchildren. 'I have two daughters, Georgina is the eldest and Cecelia is two years younger. Georgina has twins, they are fifteen, Rocco and Jay. Gia is nine. Cecelia has three kids as well: Robin, the eldest, and Sonny and Blossom, the twins. They were born during the 2007 general election campaign and came into my office on the day I was made taoiseach, in June that year.'

My mother baked for Ireland –
brown bread, soda bread, apple pies.
All those simple things in life.

Bertie admires the present generation's ability for things technical – he regularly goes to grandson Jay when he needs anything on his phone sorted. Like many of today's grandparents, he is amazed at how young kids are navigating tech, including Blossom, the youngest grandchild, who he recently watched open the games app and find Peppa Pig on the phone, without any help, aged two!

He speaks of the importance of the grandparent bond. 'I never miss a birthday party, I try to go to as many matches they're playing in as possible. Gia is a good Irish dancer, I try and go and see her. We all go to Kerry every year on holidays. From the time they were small, the kids would be out on the Kenmare river. We stay in Parknasilla, and go to Dingle and the Blaskets. My own girls were allowed on Inishvickillane when they were small, on Charlie Haughey's chopper. The Haugheys still have the island now, they would go out there in the summer still.

'Their grandmother Miriam is a hands-on granny as well. They go down to Miriam nearly every weekend. She is very good to them and she cooks for them too.

'The first and most important thing I would love for my grandchildren is for them to be healthy. If you have your health, you have your wealth. It is so important. I want them all to grow old with a healthy life. Anything is possible after that. I would love them to have a good education, and get into jobs that they enjoy. You can nearly see it already, some of them are into their sports, some art, some are more academic. I don't believe in pushing anyone anywhere, I never did that with my own kids, and I am so proud of the two girls.

'I would like to see them being good people. Cecelia always says to me that to be a good, kind person is the most important thing. I like to see them involved in activities in the school; my poor daughters are like taxi drivers, between the activities and the dancing and the football!

'I hope the world doesn't get so sophisticated that it is all about wealth and materialism. I don't think it will – in fact I think for the grandkids' generation, the four-day work week is inevitable. This decade, even. The mixture of work and leisure, the balance, it is going to be better for them than for you and me.'

Grandchildren from age fifteen to two:
Jay, Rocco, Gia, Robin, Sonny & Blossom

A Travelling Life

BERNADETTE MCDONAGH

Bernadette McDonagh, mother of four and grandparent of seven, is a member of the Traveller community. She was born in 1971 in County Westmeath 'but we weren't settled Travellers, we were in a caravan travelling around the country. We also had a wattle tent, it was made of wood and the cover was a big canvas. I loved it. We were more or less reared in the Dublin area, and we would go travelling down the country in the summer.'

The family had a hut in Avila Park in Finglas. 'There were small huts with a toilet and a hand sink, a kitchen sink, and space for a double bed, we were reared there in the winter. In the summertime we would go travelling around Limerick, Cork, all different parts of Ireland. It was a wonderful childhood. When we went off travelling, we would meet up with our cousins, you'd never be living by yourself. There were always big green fields to explore, little streams. We'd play in the big bales of straw, we would fish out little tiny fish in the streams. The older children would come with us and mind us. We'd make little tents in the fields, three little sticks covered over with a blanket or something like that. We'd play games with small stones we called 'Jack stones', and hopscotch and tip the can. The adults would be selling radios and watches and sheets and grey blankets at the side of the camps. I can barely remember that though, I was very young then.

In the summertime we would go travelling around Limerick, Cork, all different parts of Ireland. It was a wonderful childhood.

'We would travel with cars or vans, anything that had a towbar on the back of it. We would sleep in tents. Me, my sisters and my two aunts would sleep in the back of my grandfather's Escort van. They would make a little bed in the back of the van, some of us would sleep there, some of us would sleep in the trailers, and the rest would sleep in the tents. It depended on what each family had.

'Wherever we went, we absolutely loved it. The freedom of being out playing. The weather was always good back then, and the days were long. We always found something to be doing. We had one little dog called Skippy, and he came everywhere with us. But all that stopped for my family in about 1983 when we settled in a camp around the Clondalkin area, in small caravans.

'Every winter we would go back to the local school in Finglas. We were always put to the back of the class. From first class up until third class, we were given crayons and a bit of paper to keep us occupied during the Irish classes. In certain classes, we hadn't a clue what was going on, we weren't learning.

'We had a playground in school, and the settled children were put on one side of the playground and the Traveller children were put on the other. The children from the two sides had no problem interacting, they would play tig and that together. It wasn't the children's choice, it was the adult's choice. It was ridiculous. It would never happen today, they wouldn't get away with it.

'I had six pregnancies, only four survived; I had two miscarriages.

There were always big green fields to
explore, little streams. We'd play in the
big bales of straw, we would fish out
little tiny fish in the streams.

'There are a lot of Travellers now that have gone
into settled housing. We had such freedom, but most
Travellers don't have that now. They're missing out
on all the outdoor activities, the playing. They all
have phones and iPads these days. You don't see
children out playing with dollies and prams like
we did. Our Christmas presents back then were
knitting needles and yarn and we'd make hairbands
for ourselves and little dresses for our dollies with
hankies. Kids are occupied with PlayStations and
stuff now. You still see them out in the summer,
but not as much as in our summers.'

She recalls the winters as very tough. 'I
remember in 1982, the snow was very bad. My
mother and another couple of women had to walk
down to the shops because the cars couldn't move,
and some of them didn't have any transport. You'd
pull a milk crate on a rope down to the shop and put
a bag of coal in and pull it back for the fire. You'd
pick up a couple of messages. Winters were tough

for Travellers, they'd always be out trying to make a living. Some winters you'd be in the caravan, and some winters you'd be in the little huts in Avila Park.'

Bernadette had known her husband, Michael, all her life. 'Over the years, he would have gathered scrap to sell to the scrapyard. He would have worked on building sites for a while. He would have done a few different jobs, it would have varied a lot over the years.'

She was nineteen when the pair got married. 'I was young, but there were Travellers a lot younger getting married then. My own wedding was a triple wedding. My sister and my aunt got married the same day, so we had about 450 guests! We got married in the cathedral in Dundalk, and the reception was in the Carrickdale hotel near Newry. It was brilliant, a lovely day. It was so exciting planning it all and picking out what we were going to wear. It was a huge wedding, but that would not be unusual for Travellers. We didn't have a honeymoon, but that would have been common as well. I moved to Navan then, we were on the side of the road in a small caravan. There was a group of caravans there. I was well used to living in a caravan! It didn't bother me, and it still wouldn't bother me today. It was just our way of life, our way of living.'

Bernadette believes strongly in the power of holy water. 'A Traveller wouldn't go without holy water in their home. We would get it from various holy wells. We wouldn't leave the home without using the holy water. And we have blessed salt as well, that we throw around outdoors, it is more or less to keep all evil away from your home and children. You would buy the salt yourself, and there are priests who do a special blessing over the salt, and the same with the holy water. Travellers would collect bottles from Knock, Medjugorje, Lourdes, and they would pass it around to family and friends. It would always get shared around, and given to people in hospital or who were sick. If there was ever a family member sick or dying, they would give them holy water and little relics, and we would do the Rosary around the bed. From the time I was a baby, I remember holy water. I would never be let go to bed without my mother or grandmother blessing my face, and maybe saying the Rosary. I still say the Rosary. I have very good belief, to be honest. I go to mass as regularly as I can.'

I would hope that they would not be pushed aside in life, just because they are Travellers. It is getting better for Travellers, but it's getting better very slowly.

Bernadette McDonagh   33

Bernadette was only forty when she became a grandmother. 'I remember the birth of my first grandchild very well, because I was actually in the delivery suite with my daughter, with both my daughters when they were having their first. I was absolutely over the moon, it was beautiful. To have the first grandchild ... It is a different bond. It's different than having your own children. To have your own children is amazing, but there is something different about having grandchildren.

'Patrick was born on the 20th of December, so he was a lovely Christmas present to get. When a baby is born, we celebrate by wetting the baby's head and having a few drinks in the pub. Then we get ready for the christening celebration. That would be very big in some travelling families, they would make a big event out of it.'

Today Bernadette's two daughters are settled while her son lives in a caravan at the back of his grandfather's house. 'I hope that all my grandchildren get a chance in life, their full education, if that is what they want to do. School is not for everybody. There are children in all communities that school doesn't suit, but if my grandchildren can get a chance to do their full-time education and get jobs, if that is what they'd like to do, I would be happy.

'I would hope that they would not be pushed aside in life, just because they are Travellers. It is getting better for Travellers, but it's getting better very slowly. Some Travellers are becoming gardaí, so there are Travellers getting chances now. I would have left school after my confirmation. I would hope that my grandchildren would be given the chance to get the job they would like to do. I want them to be happy, relaxed in their lives. Not feeling excluded.

'I think the most important thing in life is to be treated fairly, and not to be embarrassed of who you are or where you came from. No stigma. I think that is so important. I was a shy child, kind of in myself. I felt that I wasn't good enough to do anything. But if it was now, I would have changed all of that. I would have let people know that I *was* good enough, I *am* good enough. I would have pushed myself harder than I did. I think things are easier for children today. There isn't as much discrimination.

'My grandchildren don't have much discrimination, they do be out playing with the little children in the estate, playing games with them. It was never the children who were the issue when it came to discrimination. It was always the adults and parents.'

Bernadette's extended family spans five generations. 'My grandmother, my mother, me, my daughter and my grandchild. My grandmother is eighty-six years of age. My grandfather is gone, he would have been a huge part of our lives. Knowing they are around – it is beautiful. We always take a photograph at the christenings, or whatever, of all the generations, I think that is very important. I am fifty years of age, but my grandmother is still a very important part of my life. She would ring me most days on the phone, or I would call up to her for a chat.'

Bernadette recalls her own grandfather as 'a real aul' storyteller, in jolly humour all the time. He would make us all laugh. They would always have something for us to eat, we were never left hungry.'

And her grandmother? 'She is a great woman – a survivor. She would survive on very little, she could make a living out of nothing. She had eight or ten children herself, who all had large families themselves, and she is always there for everyone. Giving advice and help and making sure we're alright. She is still in great health, flying around in great form, she still drives and is just in brilliant shape. I love having her still in my life. She loves getting visitors, she wouldn't let the grandkids leave the house without an apple or an orange or a banana or something. She loves getting pictures with them.'

And how would Bernadette like to be remembered by her own grandchildren? 'I would love my grandchildren to have good memories of me. I act the fool with them, I play funny games with them and go out and jump on the trampoline with them. I hope they have happy memories and will reminisce about me when I'm gone.'

Grandchildren from age ten to twenty months:
Patrick, Abbie, Michael, Tom, Martin,
Jacqueline & Ella

Holidays on the Farm

SEAN O'ROURKE

Broadcaster Sean O'Rourke was one of eight children born to Kevin and Mairead O'Rourke in Ratheniska, County Laois, in 1955. Their house 'backed on to a great big field where the National Ploughing Championships happened'.

'Dad was "the Master" in the local national school. He was also a great GAA man and founded the hurling club in Ratheniska. One of my earliest memories is of him coming home from a match with his glasses broken because there was a row between them and another club. I must have been about three or four at the time.'

When Sean was around five, the family moved to Galway for his father's work. 'He wanted to get a job in a university town. There were eight of us, and he believed that university education was the coming thing. But he knew he wouldn't be able to send us all away to university on a teacher's salary in the midlands, so he figured Galway would be a good shout, as we could live at home and attend the college there. He was principal of the Claddagh Boys' School from 1961 to 1975, and he died in 1977. One thing that strikes me is that I'm now older than he was when he died.'

Holidays back then were going back to farming friends of the family in Ratheniska, or to Uncle Ned and Aunt Teresa in Dunlavin, and working on the farm for ten days, alongside his siblings, five older brothers and two younger sisters.

'My uncle Ned delivered milk on a pony and trap, and myself and some of my siblings used to go around with him. The horse would fart, and we would all laugh. We would wake up at six o'clock in the morning with the racket of the milk being delivered from Premier Dairies. We would head out on the cart, all around the town and onto the terraces. We'd leave two bottles here and a half pint of cream there. People came to the door to buy Ned's milk as well. But later Ned exchanged the horse for a Renault 4 and that changed everything.

'As a child I teamed up with eight or nine other

boys and we had great freedom, playing Cowboys and Indians, war games, street football, fishing on the edge of the Corrib and picking blackberries.' The friends also spent their time robbing orchards and burning the furze. 'We often disappeared all day! We lived near the university and the hospital and they were our playgrounds too'

> My uncle Ned delivered milk on a pony
> and trap ... We would head out on the
> cart, all around the town and onto the
> terraces. We'd leave two bottles here
> and a half pint of cream there.

Sean describes a way of life in which people's expectations were very different to today. 'I grew up on the edge of Galway, in Newcastle, a middle-class suburb, and by and large I had a happy childhood, but we had a sense of not being well-off, because we were such a large family, and my mother didn't work outside the home. I didn't have a watch until I was sixteen, that is just how the world was, and I think maybe that is what is missing these days, that sense of being able to go without. The idea of going out for a meal in a restaurant or to a hotel for holidays, that was unheard of. I had two summer jobs in Market Street before I spent a summer working for the *Connacht Tribune*. It was just expected of you to go out and get a job. There was a lot of poverty around the part of Galway where my father taught.

'And I think there was a lot of stuff that we didn't realise was going on. Loveless marriages with rarely a word passing between husband and wife, one kid who had special needs who was always kept in the house, a bit of alcoholism, that sort of stuff.'

Sean's family were very religious, 'but then every family was religious back then, we had the holy water, plenty of statues and we went to mass and said the Rosary. Once a month we were marched from school to the Pro-Cathedral in Galway for confessions.' And what did he confess? 'Stealing sixpence from my mother's handbag, saying curses and fighting!'

His grandparents on his father's side had died before Sean was born, but he recalls those on the maternal side: 'They had to rear two separate families because my grandfather went to New York in the early 1920s, after having five children, and he was gone for six years, came back and had another five or six children. He went to get the money to buy a few extra acres, which they did in the end.

'My grandmother was a no-nonsense woman. My mother was in hospital one time and 'Mother from Cork', as she was called, minded us children. She ran a very tight ship. A visitor to the house gave my sister two shillings and my grandmother took it and said, "That's going to the poor, the black babies, you don't need that." I am sure she was very loving, but I was slow to notice it. My grandfather was much more gentle, he didn't say much but he was very friendly. He had a shake in his hand, and he would have the odd pint of Guinness that he would drink through a straw. He was a traditional farmer living on the side of a hill, working mainly with sheep.

'They made huge sacrifices for their children during very lean times. I'm reminded of that line Mary McAleese had about their generation: "They sank the well so we could draw the water." It's so true. I think my parents never really had a holiday. They went to Lourdes for four days in 1968 after being married for nearly twenty-five years, and that was about the height of it.'

Sean got married to Caroline Murphy and the couple have four sons and two daughters. He became a grandad in 2020 when their daughter Aisling gave birth to Saoirse. The proud grandparents went out to San Jose for Saoirse's arrival and Sean recalls holding her for the first time: 'A little bundle of joy. It was just so moving.' Then in 2022 the magic moment was repeated when their daughter Maeve gave birth to Fionn.

'You see your grandchildren in a different way to your own children. When it is your own child, the responsibility is so much greater because you know you have to rear this child, and provide for it, and it is going to be keeping you awake at night, but there is none of that with a grandchild! You just have to enjoy it.

'I hope my grandchildren will be well-rounded individuals, for them "to be men and women for others", to borrow a phrase that the Jesuits would use. I believe my children are better than I was, at the same stage. They are more responsible, better educated, harder-working. They are all so different, there are no two of them the same, as far as I can see.

'Things will be different for my grandchildren than they were for my generation, they will probably never want for anything in the material sense. That is good, provided that they appreciate what they have and don't take it for granted.

'And yet, for my own children's generation, times are harder in ways. I don't know if they will be as well-off as I now am. Both myself and Caroline had houses by the time we were thirty, that just doesn't happen now. That being said, when I had my first house, I had a milk crate as my kitchen stool, I painted the house myself, top to bottom. We had more than the bare necessities but not a huge amount more.'

Sean remembers 'a lot of religion in Galway in the sixties. The new cathedral opened, and JFK visited, and they had his picture up in the cathedral along with Patrick Pearse. Everyone went to mass back then, they had things like the Eucharistic procession. You would meet your friends – you'd go to ten o'clock mass in the cathedral and then go to play football after.

'I would want my grandchildren to have a sense of God and Christianity, and to know there is merit in having a relationship with the Lord. And loving one another and looking after their fellow human beings, that is the important thing.

'I would also love my grandchildren to be involved in sport. My main sport was rowing. It was a sport that took up six days of our lives, your free time. I didn't particularly love it but there was a great sense of camaraderie. It was a great way to learn the discipline of showing up, because you can't send seven guys out on a boat. You either have eight, or the boat can't go on the water. So you would want to be really sick to not show up! You learned about that, and about teamwork. The whole essence of rowing is literally pulling together.

'Rowing was great but it kind of fell off a cliff once you left school or college. I would love my grandchildren to do sport in a way that they would continue it in later life.'

Sean's children have grown up listening to their dad on radio, but as for his grandkids? 'They might see pictures or that, but by the time they reach secondary school, I will be well finished, I think. I had a fantastic career and I loved it, I made a little bit of ability go a long way, that's how I put it. It worked because of the people I had around me in radio.'

> I would love my grandchildren to be
> involved in sport. It is a great way to
> learn the discipline of showing up.

And his thoughts on any of his own grand-children going into journalism? 'Put it this way, I think they would have a tougher time of it than I had. Journalism used to be a career that was comparable to the civil service or the gardaí, there was a career path that you could work out for yourself, and it wasn't badly paid. Now it is far less secure. Technology has changed, everyone can be a columnist or a broadcaster now. And that has its advantages, but can you make a career from it?'

Whatever paths they take, Sean hopes that his grandchildren will live life to the full, take the chances they're given and learn to take the rough with the smooth. 'That is the essence of a good life – no regrets, or few, and enjoy it.'

Grandchildren from age two to nine months:
Saoirse & Fionn

Breaking Barriers
in a World of Men

MARY O'ROURKE

Mary O'Rourke, née Lenihan, is the erstwhile 'mammy' of Irish politics and scion of a political dynasty who served in Dáil Éireann both as a TD and a senator for thirty years. Born in 1937, Mary was given her middle names after Irish political revolutionaries Constance Markiewicz – whose home at Lissadell, Sligo was near where Mary's mother grew up – and Hanna Sheehy-Skeffington.

One of Mary's early childhood memories is of the night when, as a seven-year-old, she met then taoiseach Éamon de Valera, who was in Athlone for the general election. 'When it was over, we all went back to our house, de Valera and my father and all the Fianna Fáil lads. My sister Anne and myself were piled into bed, in our big ramshackle house. My mother said, "This is a place for men." I will never forget that.'

Every so often there was Éamon
de Valera's deep, deep voice. I would
have loved to be in there with them,
and I thought to myself, *One day
I will be in there with them.*

But Mary couldn't resist having a peep downstairs. 'I could hear all the shouting and the roaring and the laughter and glasses clinking, so I crept up the corridor. They were in the living room, a great time being had by all. I knew they wouldn't come out the door that I was at, because there was a bathroom the other side, and I know my mother would direct them there as that was the "good bathroom". So I listened and thought to myself, *What a great time they're having!* Every so often there was Éamon de Valera's deep, deep voice. I would have loved to be in there with them, and I thought to myself, *One day I will be in there with them.*

'That was an important moment for me, to know

I would want to be there, going to the meetings and talking and laughing. I always loved men's company. When I was first in cabinet, I was the only woman. We all got into Dáil Éireann the same way – and that was to get enough votes. Gemma Hussey said that when she was in cabinet, they tried to get her to make the tea! Well, they didn't try that one on me.'

Mary was the youngest in her family. Her brothers Brian and Paddy were eight and seven years older than her, her sister Anne older by five years. 'I was very much on my own, although I was very close to Paddy. I played with the other local girls, hopscotch and that sort of thing. I was a great friend of Nuala Lally whose father Martin was the station master in the Athlone train station. We were great buddies. I would ride in from the Hodson Bay [hotel] to meet her. We would read books and, in the fifties, we went to the drama festival where we made out we were very important people, selling programmes! Very important people indeed.'

Mary's parents were the hotelier owners of the Hodson Bay, Patrick Joseph Lenihan and Annie Scanlon. 'They were very good grandparents when I had my own children. My mother played bridge for Ireland. I played for a while too, but I gave it up, because it was either bridge or politics! She was a marvellous bridge player. My father not so much, but he was very into the drama.

'When I was growing up, we would always go to mass. Sometimes two masses a day! We didn't think much about it. I went to confession a lot as a child, and I would have to say, "Oh, I gave out to my mother four times!" We don't do that now. I remember my first communion. I was in a lovely dress, with a little hat, and I thought I was just gorgeous! I was collecting money, but not as much as the kids get these days! There would be holy water in every room back then. We would go up to the church with a big bottle and get a big load of it and fill up any little bottles that were vacant. That doesn't happen these days. There are hardly any priests even.

'We hung out on the street a lot, because Nuala lived in the station house so we would be out looking at the trains and counting how many people got onto one train and how many people got onto another, and all that. Very innocent! Nuala was my bridesmaid, and I was hers.

'We loved clothes, I loved shopping and buying clothes. I wasn't thrifty at all! Dunnes had begun at the time, everyone loved them. I was great at going to the shops, myself and Nuala Lally. I remember when Dunnes opened in Athlone in the seventies, down in

Irishtown. We were all delighted with the idea of it, because it was new to us. They had groceries, of course, but they had clothes as well, when no one else had clothes. We thought it was just fantastic! We would go in and buy our clothes and our underwear and our bras and all that. When I think about it, it was the first shop that you could get everything in it.

We would read books and, in the fifties,
we went to the drama festival where
we made out we were very important
people, selling programmes!

'My mother was very careful about what she wore and where she got her clothes. She managed to shop around thriftily, much more than I would. She didn't make our clothes, but there was a great dressmaker who made a lot of the clothes for my sister Anne and myself. During the war years we could still get clothes, because we would get the material and could give it to the dressmaker to make us outfits.

'Myself and Nuala used to be always chasing young fellows. I had a boyfriend, a footballer in Roscommon, but that faded away.' Then when she was eighteen, Mary met her future husband, Enda

O'Rourke, and the pair remained together through Mary's college days at UCD, after which they got engaged. 'I remember him asking me to marry him. We were at a tennis club dance in Athlone, we had a great night and it went very well. When he was leaving me home and we were canoodling and kissing he said, "Are we going to make this permanent?"

And I said, "I think we will." And that was it, we were engaged. We went to Dublin to a lovely jeweller's on Grafton Street and got my ring.'

Mary remembers every detail of her wedding in the Hodson Bay hotel. 'I have beautiful photos of it all. I wore a white dress and a beautiful veil, quite a long dress. And Enda looked gorgeous. He was a very good-looking man, until the day he died.'

The pair honeymooned in Jersey, 'which was quite a big thing to do back then. Very exotic. We went away for a week, and the night we were going away, my father P.J. Lenihan came out to say goodbye to us, and he started to cry, so I started to cry, and it was very sad! The two of us crying at leaving one another, me leaving the Hodson Bay and all that. I had a lovely life with Enda though, such a lovely life.'

Although Mary and Enda badly wanted a family, they were three years married and nothing was happening. 'So I went to see Dr Éamon de Valera [son of the politician] in Dublin. He was very nice and put me on tablets, and after six months I got pregnant with Feargal and I was delighted with myself. But then I never had number two, I waited and waited and no sign.

'I loved family life with all my heart, so I went again to Dr de Valera, and he said, "Ah, you'll have a baby," but he wasn't as fervent as he was the first time. When he first saw me he'd said, "You'll have a baby, with the love of God." I think he knew I wouldn't have another one! Number two baby never came along, so we started thinking that maybe it would be lovely to adopt, and adoption wasn't that rare, you know.'

There would be holy water in every room back then. We would go up to the church with a big bottle and get a big load of it and fill up any little bottles that were vacant.

The pair did adopt and Aengus came along when Feargal was four years old, an occasion Mary remembers with great joy.

Mary is now a grandmother of six and her

face lights up with joy when she talks about her relationship with her grandchildren. She discusses politics with all six of them, 'all the time! Aengus and Feargal were very Fianna Fáil so the kids picked that up. It's just great to have them, I am so lucky.'

Mary is very involved in her grandchildren's lives and follows their progress in school and college closely. The fact that she was minister for education from 1987 to 1991 gave her an added interest and she remembers the day she got the portfolio. 'That was the job I really loved. I admired Charlie Haughey, he gave me my first job. He called me up and said, "I'm going to make you minister for education." At that time, I was just an ordinary TD, so I said, "Oh, thank you!" I was only a beginner at that stage. It was 1982 when I first went into Dáil Éireann. I held different ministries and that, but I really loved education. I felt like you could really do some good with it.'

Becoming a minister was a highlight of her life. 'I loved education. Five years! I loved it, it was my favourite job in government. I take a lot of satisfaction from what we did, we worked very, very hard together in the department. My grandchildren loved that I was a politician: "My grandmother the minister!"

'I would be hopeful that my grandchildren would get the best education they could. I would want to watch out for them always, find out how they were doing at exams and that. My advice to them would always be to be true to themselves, to who they are, and your parents and what they taught you. Life will go very well if you stay true to yourself.

'I think things are tougher for kids today. They have to stand up to so much more, and they have to be part of a whole new world. Our world was simpler, it seemed easier than what life is now. It is much more difficult now.

'They never called me Granny, they call me Mary! And they don't ask for my advice … they just tell me what they are planning to do! I would have a great interest in what they are doing, but maybe in their own way they do ask me. I don't think they've been influenced by having a politician for a granny at all, they are all so independent.'

Mary believes in a serious work ethic. 'I think it is *highly* important to keep working,' she told me as she completed an article for her beloved bridge club in Athlone. 'I used to write about a thousand words a week, I loved doing that. I'd write little articles and I gave lectures in the colleges and I talked to people and I was loving that, I really was. I was working hard when the grandchildren were born, but I was a good granny. I was always a good granny. I loved them and they came and visited me and I visited them. They are lovely children, I adore them.'

Mary has no regrets about her devotion to politics. 'I am so glad I went into politics. My whole life was politics. I wouldn't do anything different if I could do it all again.'

Grandchildren from age twenty to eleven:
Jennifer, Sarah, Samuel, Luke, James & Scott

Our Own Front Door

JUNE CONSIDINE

Bestselling author June Considine, who writes under the name Laura Elliot, was born in Finglas, Dublin in 1945. 'My mother was a farmer's daughter from Monaghan and my father was born just outside Wexford town. He was a ship's cook and spent his working life at sea. After they married, they moved into a flat on Herbert Place and that was where I lived for the first four years of my life. Nowadays, a plaque outside the house states that it was once the summer home of the author Elizabeth Bowen.'

One of June's earliest memories is being told by her mother that they were going to move to their own house.

'At the time, Finglas was a small village but my parents' friends were convinced we were moving to the heart of the country, which we were! We moved into Finglas Park and I can still recall the excitement of knowing we now had a garden and a front door that only my own family could walk through. From what I heard as a child, Finglas Park and the surrounding houses were originally built for the Church of Ireland congregation. The houses that remained unsold were then offered for sale on the open market. As a result, I grew up in an area where Protestants and Catholics lived side-by-side, friends and neighbours, yet separated by the stern dictates of our different religions.

'As a child, I joined in all the usual games, skipping, statues, hide-and-seek, hopscotch, and various ball games. Mainly, I played with my friends in Finglas Woods, just outside the village. Today, the woodland is buried under a busy shopping centre but back in the day, we climbed trees and made dams in the little river that ran through the woods. My strongest memories are of racing through sun-dappled trails and hanging upside down from the branches.

'I went to school in Finglas and loved English, especially writing essays. Friends insist that they remember me standing up in class reciting poems I'd written yet I've no strong memory of doing so.

Becoming a writer in those days was a dream to me, never a reality. I thought of writers as "other people". They wrote the books and I read them avidly. I'm still a passionate reader and no longer have to dream about being a writer.'

June met her future husband, Seán, when friends organised a blind date. He worked in insurance and was a singer in a rock band. He came down from the stage one night and told June that he was dedicating the next song to her. It was the Elvis Presley hit "Can't Help Falling in Love".

'That was a very special moment that will never for forgotten,' she recalls. 'It sealed the deal and four years later we were married.'

I can still recall the excitement of knowing
we now had a garden and a front door that
only my own family could walk through.

Sadly, though, her mother, Bridie Bolger, would never get to meet June's firstborn, Tony, as she died unexpectedly, after surgery for a brain tumour, within five months of her daughter's wedding.

'My beautiful mother was still a young woman, vibrant, special, and so loved. It was a time of heartbreak for our family. When I called in to see her at the hospital one evening shortly before her operation, she asked if I was pregnant. It was still early days but I was looking pale and tired, and she picked up on the signs immediately. At least I was able to share the news with her but it has been one of the saddest regrets of my life that she never experienced the joy of being a grandmother.'

June and Seán have three children and four grandchildren – Romy, Ava, Nina and Seán (Jr) – aged from eighteen down to two. 'Seánie is the youngest, our first grandson, and after three granddaughters, he is a whole new and wonderful experience. His energy is high octane! His sister Nina has a delightful imagination and tells me she wants to be a writer when she grows up.

'I had the privilege of being present at the birth of Romy, my first grandchild. In that instant, I knew what it was like to be a grandmother. It was an immediate and overwhelming feeling of happiness and protectiveness. Being a grandmother is delightful. How can I describe it? I feel the same sensations of cherishing, loving and protecting my grandchildren that I experienced with my own children, but not the huge responsibility that comes with parenting. When I say goodbye to them at the end of the day, I can relax down into the nearest armchair, knowing that they are going back into safe, loving hands.

'When my daughter Ciara's children, Romy and Ava, were younger, we looked after them one day a week. We collected them from playschool, primary school, and secondary school. We have kept up that closeness over the years and Seán has always been actively involved in their care. He adores being a grandfather and has a fantastic relationship with all of them. He has quite interesting conversations with them about their lives on the school drives. They are lovely open children. We now follow that same routine with Michelle's children, Nina and Seán, and, hopefully, we'll also see them through their schooling. Our time with them is precious.

'We have holidayed with our grandchildren from the very beginning, and that has played a huge part in our lives. Every year we go to Ballyferriter in west Kerry. They love that holiday and our older grandchildren, who are wonderful singers and musicians, have sung from a young age in one of the local pubs. West Kerry has been hugely influential on them and it's great to be a part of that.

'Sadly, with my mother's early passing, my children had only one grandmother to spoil them.

Kay Considine was a force of nature, a strong, independent woman who loved to sing and enjoy a party. She had a great sense of mischief and didn't suffer fools gladly. All my children have inherited her love of song and will never say no to a hooley, especially at Christmas time.

'When I was a child, my father always tried to get home from the ship to spend Christmas with us. He cooked Christmas dinner and we spent a quiet day at home. I was the eldest of four, with one sister and two brothers, and we played with our new toys in what we called the "sitting room" – which was seldom used throughout the year – while my parents spent precious time together in the dining room. Eventually, we'd be called in to dinner and then it was back to the toys, the books and the records until bedtime.

'When I met Seán, all that changed. The Considine Christmas was a livelier affair, with big extended family gatherings and lots of singing. I inherited the 'Christmas party' shortly after our marriage! Every Christmas night, when our relatives from both families had finished their celebrations, they would gather late at our house to sing and play music until the early hours. The tradition of the hooley lives on, an inter-generational gathering, and it's wonderful to know it's in safe hands with the younger generation.'

When asked how life is for the upcoming

generation, June says, 'Every generation creates their own particular style and culture, and their era may seem different and strange to us, even grim. As we know, the challenges they face on an environmental level are unprecedented.

> If I wanted to pass anything on to
> my grandkids, it would be kindness,
> open-mindedness, the courage to be
> different, and the confidence to believe
> in themselves and their abilities.

'But there are many opportunities too, and I marvel at the development of the internet, and at the range of careers that are possible for young people nowadays. However, I do think they are under massive pressure regarding the online world. The influence of advertising and social media is huge. That's a difficulty I didn't have as a child. It was a more innocent life, a much simpler time.

'If I wanted to pass anything on to them it would be kindness, open-mindedness, the courage to be different, and the confidence to believe in themselves and their abilities. I hope they will have a strong sense of themselves and won't be cowed by bullying, be it physical or cyber. I hope they can deal with anxiety in a world where so many demands are made on them. Those demands are often vacuous and formed by celebrity culture and influencers. I wish their strong family ties will always remain so. I hope they can dream and channel that dream into a realistic form, and cope with disappointment if it comes their way.

> My grandmother said, 'Look, this exam is not important. What is important is that I am here with you now and I love you and believe you are very special.'

'They already display many of those traits and I'm very proud of their independence and talents. No doubt they don't tell us everything that goes on in their lives and that's to be expected. I believe they will have more confidence than I did, and more opportunities. They will also have a more rounded education. I went to a graduation evening when Ava had finished her Transition Year and the pupils were presented with their certificates. Many young people stood up and spoke about that year, the different projects they undertook, the charity work they did, the excursions they took, and many other TY experiences. They were full of confidence and promise.

'I hope my grandchildren will remember me with fondness. As someone who was funny, and kind, and loved them passionately. I have an abiding memory of my own grandmother, who was from Monaghan. When I was a child, I failed an exam during one of her visits to us. I was thirteen at the time and was convinced I'd never recover from the shame of this failure. I remember going to a river near my home and crying my eyes out on the river bank. I heard my name being called and when I looked up my grandmother was standing there. My mother, who guessed that something was wrong, had sent her out to search for me. My grandmother took me in her arms and comforted me.

'She said, "Look, this exam is not important. What is important is that I am here with you now and I love you and believe you are very special." I remember it so vividly, her words always stayed with me – along with that sense of what it is to be a grandmother. To be there during the hard times, with a big hug.'

Grandchildren from age eighteen to two:
Romy, Ava, Nina & Seán

Ireland's Favourite Granda

IAN MCELHINNEY

Ian Stephenson McElhinney – or 'Granda Joe' to a nation of viewers of *Derry Girls* – was born in Belfast on 30 June 1948. He has clear memories of early childhood, including a day when he 'fell off a slippery chair, and banged my chin on the hearth. I had to get a stitch in my chin. I was quite young at that stage.'

Then there were the high jinks. 'We were two brothers, so we would be out in the back garden kicking a ball around and riding a bike when we were a bit older. My dad had a vegetable plot in the back garden, and we used to dig that up and literally throw mud at each other! Very young children love mess. My youngest grandchild, Etta, is just twenty months old, and she will be eating with a spoon, and she'll think, *Sod this!* and put her hands in and feed herself that way instead. If it goes down her wee front, so be it, they love mess!

'I used to go out to an aunt of mine in Donegal, and I loved feeding the chickens there. She gave them corn in the evenings, but in the mornings she gave them a mash of potatoes and eggshell and bits of wholemeal – a whole smattering of things that she would have thrown in and mashed it all up. I used to love nothing more than mashing up that mess and going out and scattering it to the birds.'

My dad had a vegetable plot in the back garden, and we used to dig that up and literally throw mud at each other!

Ian says he had 'no interest' in acting until he was about fifteen and did a school play. But despite pursuing it as a hobby through his college years and after, Ian was thirty before he decided to leave the day job of teaching and try acting as a career. 'In those days you had to get an equity card. I had been out of Northern Ireland for thirteen years at this stage, with no intention of going back, or at least

I thought that. I was told that the best way to get an equity card was to go back to your roots. At this stage the Troubles were well established, it was the late seventies. Bizarrely, with my decision to be an actor, I ended up back in Belfast. That was fine for a couple of years, I kept getting work here so I stayed put, even though I thought I would be better off in London.'

He met his wife Marie Jones in 1980, during a production of a play called *Feiffer's People*, and the pair married ten years on. 'Marie had one child already from a previous marriage, so I have a grown-up stepson, and then we have two of our own. They're all boys, Darren, Matthew and David.'

> I used to go out to an aunt of mine
> in Donegal, and I loved feeding the
> chickens there. She gave them corn
> in the evenings, but in the mornings
> she gave them a mash of potatoes
> and eggshell and bits of wholemeal.

Ian and Marie have three grandchildren. 'Our first grandchild was Jacob, Darren's child, followed by Daisy. Becoming a grandfather is a rather special thing. We have Etta now, Matthew's child, and we are very hands-on there. She stays over, we have to get up in the middle of the night, changing her and feeding her, taking her to nursery, taking her outdoors, wheeling her in the pram through the park and all that.

'The main thing you want for your grandchildren is to have no major health issues. Going forward from that, you want their lives as little challenged in that regard. Of course with a bit of luck they will have a long life, and an interesting life. You want them to be engaged with the world and that they will have an interesting time. With a bit of luck, they will spend their lives working at something that gives them pleasure as opposed to having to be done, and that they get some sort of stimulation from the work they do.

'As long as I'm around, I want to do the best I can at looking after them, and when I'm not around, to do the best I can in protecting them. I think they have a much tougher life than I did. You can argue that they have so much now that I didn't have at their age. I wore hand-me-downs as a kid, from my older brother, and we didn't have all the electronics and gadgetry and mobile phones that they have now. What we did was go out and play, enjoyed the outdoors. Oftentimes if you were indoors, your dad would say, "What are you doing in here, away outside to play!" Nowadays kids are much more indoor-centred, because of all the gadgetry. Which is interesting in its own right, but I don't think it is particularly healthy.

'I think they should be outdoors enjoying the fresh air and nature, friendship and face-to-face contact. That is why Covid has been so awful for kids, because it has denied them all that. Being face-to-face with people is so important, and I think all this technology and being able to do everything remotely – I hate the fact that it could take over.

'I remember reading a book once, and I came across a great line: "Opportunity doesn't do home visits." I have said that to the kids, never mind the grandkids, all along. You have got to get out there and make your own way. Simply by getting out there, things happen. People who get out there and engage and are willing to meet people, things happen to them. Don't hide indoors. I want them to be confident enough to go out in the world and meet people. They will happen upon opportunities that way.

'I hope my grandchildren will remember me as someone who said something of value to them at some point. *Actually, he was alright. He said this to me, and now that I think of it, that was useful.* You don't know what they are picking up and then they scare you by picking up far too much!'

> I had been out of Northern Ireland for thirteen years at this stage ... I was told that the best way to get an equity card was to go back to your roots. At this stage the Troubles were well established, it was the late seventies.

As for Ireland's best-loved screen grandfather, Ian says he is loving playing the role. 'The thing about Granda Joe is that yes, he is a huffy bollocks, and yes, he gives Gerry a hard time, but the bottom line is that he's got daughters and granddaughters and he is so protective to his womenfolk. He loved his wife, that comes through in a few lovely moments. He is very much a man who loves the women in his life. When it comes to Gerry, somehow he has slipped in there – so he just has to be watched and occasionally put in his place, so he knows what the score is! It almost becomes a running joke between the two of them.'

Ian has no intention of retiring from acting. 'I will keep working; I am at official retirement age, but I have no interest in retiring. As long as I am fit enough, I will carry on doing it; I enjoy it and I don't want to give it up. If you want to stop working, absolutely, and why shouldn't you? But if you have a job that you love, like I do, you want to keep going. It keeps the mind alert and the body active and I am delighted to be doing it.'

And Ian has this advice for parents and grand-parents: 'Enjoy your children and your grandchildren as much as you can, because they keep changing and every stage is so different. I suppose if I am honest, to me they are most interesting when they are really, really wanting to find out about things, their natural inquisitiveness comes at about seven or eight. When that comes, you want to encourage that and keep encouraging right through their teens. You want them to never be scared to ask a question. When they are wee, they never *stop* asking questions, but you want to keep that going. That is how you learn. Curiosity is a great thing in kids and needs to be encouraged.'

Grandchildren from age thirteen to twenty-two months:
Jacob, Daisy & Etta

Cycling to Terenure
with a Union Jack

CEDRIC BAILEY

A standout memory from the early life of Cedric Bailey, who was born in 1932, concerns his schooldays at the preparatory school on Rathgar Road. 'I didn't go to school until I was six, I'm not sure why, but I was very proud of the fact that I hadn't missed a day's school until, at age eight, my family dog bit me.

'The infection was moving up my arm and they were about to cut it off, apparently, it was that serious. But my mother persuaded them to wait. It was the early days of penicillin. I remember the incident well. I had come home from school, and I was petting him, and he just turned on me. My mother brought me down to the hospital and left a note for my father – "Mind the dog, it has gone mad." He didn't see the note and took it out for a walk! The dog was only a small thing, but it gave a big bite. I still have the scar. Luckily, I still have my arm too!

> At age eight, my family dog bit me.
> The infection was moving up my arm
> and they were about to cut it off,
> apparently, it was that serious. But
> my mother persuaded them to wait.
> It was the early days of penicillin.

'I was very annoyed that I had to miss two days of school and break my record, I was hoping to get a prize.'

Another early memory was of roller-skating up and down the road outside his home on Fortfield Terrace in Rathmines. 'The skates would clip onto your shoes, and they ruined the shoes!

'Then I remember the day war was declared in 1939, and being told to keep quiet please, as my father was trying to listen to the radio. I wasn't the most biddable child, apparently. My brother was very good and calm, but I used to make a lot of noise. I remember the end of the war better than the beginning. I recall cycling down to Terenure with the Union Jack, and a load of yobbos knocked me off my bike! I don't know why I was waving it, something to do with the victory at the end of the war.

'I had two brothers, Ian and Don, and one sister, Rhona. Both brothers are dead now but I still have my sister. Ian became a well-known neuro-surgeon and was part of a pioneering team that invented a method of inserting metal plates to repair gunshot wounds to the head during the Troubles in the North.'

Cedric recalls working life for his father in the 1930s, who was an early pioneer of the recycling business in Ireland.

'Dad was a commercial traveller for a company called Reckitts. They were in Rathfarnham. When the war started, he had no car, so they offered him an indoor job with a lower salary, which he couldn't really afford, because he had four young children at that stage. He was introduced to this English chap who was sent over to run a paper mill, and they were chatting, and he was saying that he didn't know what he was going to do for raw material. In those days they were making paper from straw, strawboard. He said he was very short of raw material and any old wastepaper would be good and that's how my father got into recycling. His first customer was Bank of Ireland, repulping some of the old ledgers in the basement of the bank.'

As to the career path for a young middle-class Irish boy of the time, Cedric recalls college days, and a heart that was more at home in the family business than in the academic world.

'When I left school, I was really undecided what I wanted to do. My elder brother was studying medicine and I thought maybe I should follow him. Another school friend said that my father would love me to join him in the business. I thought, "That will do me!" We called the business J.R. Bailey Limited, which was my father's name. Dad wanted me to go to Trinity, so I did for a while, studying industrial relations, but my heart wasn't in it. I wanted to get on with the business. I really loved it, all my life. Although we were at the forefront of recycling in Ireland, we weren't conscious of it back then. We were just reusing paper. We had to sort it out into different grades and take out brass fasteners and pins and that. The pulping machines were fairly primitive at the time. I remember when the machines got magnets, so we were allowed to leave pins in, and the excitement! That would have been very advanced for the 1950s.'

I remember the day war was declared in
1939, and being told to keep quiet please, as
my father was trying to listen to the radio.

Cedric Bailey and Jill Barrett met when they were fifteen and fourteen respectively. 'We were in a co-ed school, Newtown School in Waterford, and we "clicked". "Clicking" was a phrase back then for having a girlfriend. My parents wouldn't have been aware at that stage. We didn't "go out" as such, it was a boarding school, and we didn't go out of the grounds! We would go for nice walks in the woods. The teachers knew. It would have been common in school. Not everybody would have stayed together and got married, but quite a few did, I think.

'I left school before Jill did, and had a few girlfriends in the two years before we got together again. She went to Cathal Brugha Street to study catering and then her first job was in a school in Wales. That only lasted about a term, it was slave labour almost. She came back and got a job as the housekeeper in Trinity for the provost and his wife. She had a lovely flat in the house there.

'We got married in our early twenties and went to Majorca for our honeymoon, which was very exotic at the time. It was a big deal to travel abroad in those days; kids of today would find it hard to understand, many of them have their first plane journey when they're too small to even remember it. Not so then.'

One by one the kids came along, Lynn, Deborah and twins Andrew and Nicholas. 'We were pretty hands-on parents but I often regret not spending *more* time with the children when they were small. Work took up so much time. But in 1959, when our second daughter, Deborah, was born, I did just that, and we came down to Wicklow for the summer and rented a house in Brittas Bay. It cost twenty pounds a week, and we said, "Never again will we pay that!"

'Then we found a house for sale near Brittas in 1960, ideal for a summer home. We eventually bought it for nine hundred pounds. I arranged an overdraft of three hundred pounds in the bank. When we first bought it, we had water, electricity and a toilet but that was about it.

'The family would all come down and spend the whole summer there. I was driving a Morris Minor at the time, and with four children and two dogs that was quite a trek! I was working but I would come down every Wednesday and every weekend, and it always seemed to be wet! We would spend our days on the beach with the children, getting sand in the sandwiches.

'I remember using milk bottles for boiled eggs, because we had no egg cups! At summer's end we would lock up for winter and head back to Dublin. And when we'd return before Easter, the walls would be streaming with damp. We would light the fires and hang up the bedclothes to deal with it.'

And each summer there would be the influx of friends from Dublin. 'Few people had holiday homes at that time so we'd have great hooleys, simple though, where the food would be boiled eggs and soda bread. When too many people arrived down, they slept in tents in the garden, there were a lot of people! I have very happy memories of those days. The house was probably the best investment we ever made, we're still using it today.'

Years later, with his own family grown, Cedric was delighted to become a grandfather. 'I have no memories of my grandmothers; both of them were dead before I was born. I didn't have a close relationship with my grandfathers, I missed out on that, so I cherish the relationship I have with my grandchildren.

'I was only forty-nine or fifty when I became a grandad, when my daughter Lynn gave birth to Hannah and later her sisters Elspeth and Ruth. The first time we met Hannah was a week after she was born. I was trusted to hold her, but I was nervous to meet this tiny thing. A very precious moment, just as it was for each of them when they came along.'

Now Cedric has seven great-grandchildren: Toby, Miriam and Chris are Hannah's children; Susanna and Jacob are Elspeth's children, and Joel and Freddie are the sons of Ruth.

> I recall cycling down to Terenure with the Union Jack, and a load of yobbos knocked me off my bike! I don't know why I was waving it, something to do with the victory at the end of the war.

'I think my grandchildren and great-grand-children have harder lives than we had. We didn't have a huge amount of money, but we were always comfortable, and we didn't have the worries that the present generation have, between social media and availability of drugs and alcohol. We never really drank growing up. My mother would have a sherry at Christmas, that was the extent of her drinking. We were never really in the pubs.

'In terms of religion, we would have been very influenced by the Quaker tradition from our school-days and I would have been involved in it ever since. I wasn't brought up a Quaker, but my grandmother was. I think she would have changed when she "married out", as it was called – she married a Church of Ireland chap. In general, religion was taken much more seriously in those days, although numerous of my own grandchildren are devoutly religious.

'I think my grandchildren don't have the freedom that I had, the freedom to go out without worrying about getting mugged. I know people don't walk down O'Connell Street much at night anymore, whereas I wouldn't have given it a thought.

'There are a lot of opportunities for young people these days, particularly girls, that weren't there when I was growing up. When Jill and I were first married, she went to join the library, and she wasn't allowed because officially, she was a chattel of mine and I had to sign a library application for her. She never really went to the library after that, she went in and bought books instead. She was very fond of reading. Once a week she went into the city, and she nearly always came home with books for the children.'

Sadly, Cedric lost his wife of sixty-six years, on 11 April 2022. 'I miss Jill. It is probably the most awful thing that has happened me. We had a very happy and long life together.'

Cedric wishes that his grandchildren would be 'as happy as Jill and myself were, either in their married or unmarried lives. I would wish that they would be successful in whatever they do. I think I have had a very lucky life. Everything has worked out very well. With marriage, with work, with children and grandchildren.

'I would like to be remembered as someone who influenced my grandchildren in how to carry on with their life. Memories were always important, both to me and Jill. She compiled a book of family memories … and I suppose I will be living on memories now. I would be very happy as long as the grandchildren don't think of me as a blathering old eejit, which I hope I am not!'

Grandchildren from age thirty-nine to twenty-seven:
Hannah, Elspeth, Janek, Ruth,
twins Daniel & Luke, & Sam

Generations of Cloth Cutters

LOUIS COPELAND

Louis Copeland is the grandson of a Jewish tailor, Hyman Copeland, who came to Ireland from Lithuania in 1910. Apparently, Hyman thought he was on a ship bound for New York but it docked in Cork, where he disembarked anyway and started the Copeland dynasty. He then moved to live in Dublin and met an Irish girl, Harriot McCarthy, and became a Catholic. The couple had two children, Louis (Snr) and Rachel.

Louis Copeland's father married May Kearney and they had five children, the second of whom is the Louis at the heart of this piece. He grew up in Drumcondra in Dublin and tailoring was in his blood from very early on, a business he has now been in for over sixty years.

'From the age of ten or eleven I used to get the bus into town and go down to my father on Capel Street and work there in the afternoon. I would do that three or four days a week, sweep the floor, make the tea, pull the tacks out of the suits, that kind of stuff. I think I must have loved it because it was something to do and you got a few bob that helped as well.'

But there was plenty of time for games too. 'I lived facing St Joseph's School for the Blind. We used to play on the grounds there. It was run as a farm, you would think you were in the middle of the country, you would smell the cattle and the horses. That's where we grew up.'

Louis says his mother was a religious woman and they all went to Sunday mass and said the Rosary.

Louis left school at fourteen to pursue his dream of being a tailor, attending Parnell Square Technical School for tailoring and textiles. 'I did two years there training as a tailor and then I went to work in The Two Owls as an apprentice. My memory of working in the factory was you had to be in at eight o'clock in the morning. Now, eight o'clock in the morning, fifty years ago, was like six o'clock in the morning now and my uncle used to give me a lift. He worked in the printing factory in Dolphin's Barn so he would collect me at seven thirty in the morning and bring me over to High Street. You had to be in at eight o'clock sharp to clock in with your card. If you were even five minutes late you had to wait outside until nine o'clock! It made you punctual in the future so it kind of sticks in your memory – you have to be on time or else you get your hour docked. You could be standing out in the rain for nearly an hour until you got in.'

From the age of ten or eleven I used to get the bus into town and go down to my father on Capel Street and work there in the afternoon. I would do that three or four days a week, sweep the floor, make the tea, pull the tacks out of the suits, that kind of stuff.

Clothes fifty years ago lasted longer. 'The fabrics were heavier and people would often "turn" a coat to give it another few years. But you always knew if a coat had been turned because the breast pocket and the lapel hole were on the other side.'

The factory closed down and Louis went to work with his father. 'It was a natural progression and we had a good bond working together.' But, he says, tailoring has changed a lot over the years. 'It's not really tailoring as such now, it's retailing. Tailors are in the background. It would be more retail clothing, casual wear, overcoats, coats, and jackets. It is totally different now.' And do men wear suits as much today as they used to? 'Obviously in the last couple of years they weren't but there is a swing back to it now, they are starting to come back. There's a lot of weddings going on at the moment, with weddings being cancelled for the last two and a half years, so that's been good for us.' Louis' son, also Louis, will eventually take over the business and Louis hopes that one of his grandchildren may follow. 'It's a bit early to tell but probably. Hopefully!'

Louis particularly remembers 1963 when he was fourteen years old 'and the Beatles were playing in the Adelphi and George Harrison's uncle or cousin lived in Drumcondra and I remember waiting to see if I could get a glimpse of George at the time, I probably waited for the afternoon, but he never turned up!'

Then forty-eight years ago, Louis met his future wife, Mary Murphy, a nurse in St Vincent's hospital. He vividly remembers the arrival of his own three children, Louis Jnr, Avril and Rachel. 'Husbands today go in with their wives to have the baby with them. I remember when my first son was born in

Holles Street. In those days you would have one car and you wouldn't have a telephone at home and I remember collecting my wife a couple of days after the baby was born and bringing them home and staying for a cup of tea and I would go back to work at two thirty. They were different times, I mean there was no parental leave for a week. I had parental leave for probably an hour and a half!'

I went to work in The Two Owls as an apprentice. My memory of working in the factory was you had to be in at eight o'clock in the morning ... If you were even five minutes late you had to wait outside until nine o'clock!

The arrival of Louis' first grandchild was 'exciting, and they named him Louis so that's kind of special'. He is close to his grandchildren. 'They come down every week and we have Sunday lunch, most Sundays.'

Looking back on his own childhood, Louis says, 'I hear people talking about nuns and giving out about them now but personally I think nuns did a fantastic job, I just think they are great people.

There were a few bad apples but generally, I think these people devoted their life to helping other people and just for a few bad apples people have a bad opinion of religion. When you think about the nuns running hospitals, they did it with precision. I hate when I hear people giving out about the nuns and the priests.'

Louis believes it's important to be courteous. 'I think it is very important to respect people. You go into a restaurant and you see people at a table and they don't even look up when the waiter or waitress comes to take their order. That kills me, I have to say, because it could be my grandchild or whoever serving, and respect is very important. I would like my grandchildren to have that sense of respect.'

> The fabrics were heavier and
> people would often 'turn' a coat
> to give it another few years."

Louis, for whom retirement is nowhere on the cards, believes that life is more challenging for his grandchildren than it was for his generation. 'It's probably more complicated insofar as when I was a kid we just went out and played football on the road, now they are faced with technology and I worry sometimes when I see the grandchildren on phones and playing games, I would prefer them to be out on the road. I think sport is very important for children to keep them occupied. I worry sometimes they get too caught up in technology. Obviously I would like them all to be working, I would like them to be respectful, make sure they look after their mother and father, look after their grandfather!'

Grandchildren from age sixteen to one:
Louis, Sophie, Harry, Charlie, Anna, Sebastian & Dan

Watching Wildlife
Along the Dodder

DON CONROY

Don Conroy taught Ireland's children of the 1980s and 1990s how to draw, with his much-loved slot on RTÉ's flagship kids' programme *Dempsey's Den*, later *The Den*. He grew up in the 1950s in Donnybrook in Dublin and spent his time as a youngster watching kingfishers and other wildlife in Herbert Park and along the Dodder river, 'but what really kicked off my interest in wildlife was when I was nine years old. My mother told me that my Aunt Lizzie was "a little bit sick" and was in hospital. She wanted me to make her a nice get well card. I found out her favourite bird was a robin, so I did a cartoon drawing of a robin singing outside a hospital window, and a woman inside with a thermometer in her mouth. She loved it!

Aunt Lizzie had entered my drawing in a competition, and the book I won was called *Wildlife of Britain and Ireland*. I got first place under-twelves, so that was very exciting. In that book there were loads of beautiful illustrations of wildlife.

'About a month later I got this parcel in the post, and it turns out Aunt Lizzie had entered my drawing in a competition, and the book I won was called *Wildlife of Britain and Ireland*. I got first place under-twelves, so that was very exciting. In that book there were loads of beautiful illustrations of wildlife.' And so Don's passion for drawing wildlife was sealed, and his future direction set, aided by his mother's keen support.

'I lived near the cinema, the Sandford cinema in Ranelagh. When I was young, everyone went to the cinema regularly and I used to come back all excited, after seeing this film or that film, and my mother would say, "Why don't you draw a picture and explain it?" My mother encouraged me and I was drawing from the age of four; Bridget Conroy was her name. My father died when I was six months old, so I never knew him. Mum always supplied me with paper and pencils. When I wrote to Santa Claus, looking for bikes and all kinds of stuff, I would get watercolour sets and paper; I used to say, "How does Santa Claus know?"'

Don recalls childhood games of cowboys and Indians, a favourite of the era. 'I always wanted to be an Indian but my friend was always like, "You can't be an Indian, you've got blond hair!" So I was always General Custer, with twenty of my friends jumping on me and beating me up!'

He was the youngest of five children and remembers his mother as 'an amazing woman who had a hard job. She had a quiet charm and worked in what was then the local pharmacy. I remember one day, when I was about six, coming home from school, and there was an ambulance outside my house. I saw my mother going into it, and it was such a shock. There was nobody in the house and I just ran into the park ... I asked God, "If my mother dies, let me die with her." I was so frightened. She survived though and came home.

'My Aunt Lizzie, who was living in County Laois, came up and minded us. It was very interesting getting to know this woman from the country, all her country ways and her great sense of humour. Whenever we visited Aunt Lizzie she used to hide small sums of money around the house and told me the fairies leave it when special people come to visit. She ran the post office in Ballacolla so she had all the local news and yarns.

'Aunt Lizzie loved the cinema but rarely got to go, except when she stayed with us in Dublin. So she and my mother would go almost every single night!'

Don's first real job was as a graphic artist in an advertising agency. He went to art college by night and then he went to George Colley, an artist who taught portraiture and fine art.

He met his wife, Gay Neary, while they were both playing in *The Playboy of the Western World* with MPC Productions in The Eagle in Glasthule. He was Christy Mahon. 'It was a long trek but Gay was living in Belgrave Square in Rathmines, and she had a Honda 50, and she used to ask if I wanted a lift. So that was how we clicked.'

They got married in 1976 and had five children. 'Sarah was our first child, then there was Richard, David, Sophie and Justine. They all were in steps! I remember the first time I gazed upon Sarah. She was born in the Rotunda hospital, and I couldn't believe the beauty of her. She had really blonde hair. I was there for the birth, it was something else. I walked back to Donnybrook from there, it was sort of raining lightly, and I wanted to tell the world. It was amazing, a new kind of love that I didn't know existed. It was extraordinary.'

Don and Gay's first grandchild, Aindriú, was born twenty-seven years ago and Don says, 'The first time I held him was the same feeling that I had when his mum, Sarah, was born. I had such a strong bond with him, and I still do. I have nine grandchildren now and the extraordinary thing about being a grandad … I didn't have a father figure, of course, but I used to fantasise … anyone could have been my father, artists that lived four hundred years ago; I was trying to pick the best out of all these wonderful people who existed as role models.

'My experience with people who talked about their grandfathers was that there was a big distance for a lot of them. "He's a bit grumpy at times," that sort of thing, "He was always a distant figure." I thought to myself, *I'm not going to be like that*. The whole country calls me Don, because of RTÉ's *The Den*. So I decided that they could call me Don too!

'I do lots of drawing with my grandchildren. They'd come in after playing games, or to get food, and I would say, "Look at this," and draw a big circle, and they'd draw it too, and then I'd say, "Will we make that an eye?" and then suddenly we would be drawing together. I never wanted to make it an official thing, because a lot of people would tell me they had been put off music because of it being too strict. We made it fun!'

> I didn't have a father figure, but I used to fantasise … anyone could have been my father, artists that lived four hundred years ago.

On how life today compares to when he was young, Don says, 'Children today are growing up in a very different world. The most important thing is to be there for them. To be a source of strength, wisdom and fun. To show them the importance of being enthusiastic about life. To know that no matter what their problems are, they can feel like they can talk. If they feel isolated in life, they can be very vulnerable to other influences. That is why families are so important. People who are on their own for the most part can be very vulnerable.

'I was lucky enough to grow up in an area like

Donnybrook, where everybody looked out for you. There was a sense of community spirit, everybody made sure everyone else was okay. Everyone was kind of my uncle, my aunt. That has gone, that's not around anymore. People are working so late, such long hours. Housing estates are empty most of the day, people have to buy alarms and security systems. There is a lot of fear in society these days, which is a shame, because fear disempowers you. It makes you afraid of life. We should be valuing this great journey that is life. I probably sound quite weird on chat shows because I try and speak from that perspective. I am not trendy, or in fashion, with the zeitgeist.

> Everybody looked out for you. There was
> a sense of community spirit, everybody
> made sure everyone else was okay.
> Everyone was kind of my uncle, my aunt.

'Religion was very serious when I was growing up. I think it's a shame that religion is almost non-existent now, we're a post-Christian society in some ways. The value of having Christian ethics, a Christian background, the cultural and mystical side, it is a pity it is gone. It is not just rules and regulations, which people think it is. It has been spoiled by bad behaviour by certain priests. Cutting yourself off from an understanding of the transcendental, the creator, God, whatever name you put on it — it is a shame to make that disconnect, because then it is just about us wandering around the Earth and bumping into each other.

'I would hope that my grandchildren will have more peace on this planet. That people will have more tolerance for each other and value each other, different cultures … I would hope they would never try to be someone they are not. Regarding Ireland, I would hope they would have a cultural awareness and value our rich history.

'I would like them to be content in life, meet partners if they want that, and continue on the great tradition of life. It is important to have a core value, whether people agree with it or not. You have to have a hurt-free attitude. And I would like my grandchildren to remember me as someone who complemented life.'

Grandchildren from age twenty-seven to four:
Andriú, Alannah, Aviyah, Violet, Naomi, Leora,
Ryan, Fionn & Cian

Keeping the Faith

RUTH BOAL

Growing up in Wales and England before moving to Dublin, the earliest memories of Ruth Boal centre around her grandmother, Amelia Dutton, or 'Nain', who had a little cottage on the Welsh coast, where Ruth and her sister regularly visited. 'Breeze Cottage was in a gorgeous spot, idyllic. It had a very flowery garden, I can remember the smell of the gorse. We were allowed to go out and about playing in the gorse bushes, the yellow of them! It was dark indoors and she had a case of medals awarded to past family members.

'She was a lady. She used to wear tweed and buy things from Fortnum & Mason in London. And we used to get big Easter eggs from her at Easter.'

Ruth was seven when the family left Wales and

went to live in Braintree in Essex, at that point a small market town, but growing from a London influx. 'My mum's mum, Granny, was in Essex and we visited her every Saturday, when she always had a little paper bag of sweets waiting for us. We lived in a cul de sac, and we had lots of friends on the road. We would play games – hopscotch and skipping – and cycle our bikes. I quite liked being inside. I remember the knock on the door and "Is Ruth coming out to play?" and I wouldn't want to be disturbed – I was too busy compiling my next magazine!

> Nain was a lady. She used to
> wear tweed and buy things from
> Fortnum & Mason in London.

'My mum, Kathleen, let us play a lot. We made tents in the house and did a lot of reading and writing. I made little magazines and books. I loved books – Enid Blyton, *The Railway Children*, *Thursday's Child* … all the Malory Towers books. I loved all those. I never wanted anything to go wrong though, I would always skip the parts I didn't like!

'I also loved my dolls and doll houses. We didn't

have a TV, my parents didn't want one. But I used to try and wangle that I would go over to someone's house if there was some TV series on that I would want to watch.'

Ruth likes to think of herself as Irish because her father was born in Dublin. 'He died last year, aged ninety-three. Dad was a radio operator for the ships. His father was Catholic and Irish, and his mother was English and Protestant.'

> We didn't have a TV, my parents didn't want one. But I used to try and wangle that I would go over to someone's house if there was some TV series on that I would want to watch.

Ruth and her three sisters grew up in a religious household, and she went on to marry a Presbyterian minister, Alan. 'My parents were both Christians, my father was brought up Catholic, but once he was in Wales he was in the Church of Wales with my mum. He had books on the saints, and he was strict in his religious beliefs, whereas my mother was a little softer. They had a little Bible study group in the house. We went to the services and once, at the feet-washing ritual at Easter, I shouted out, "I want my feet washed!"

'I don't really like the term "religious", it was more of a way of life. When we were in Wales, we were in a small-village type of church, and when we went to England it was much more up and coming, a community-type church, with sales of work and meals together, various clubs and all that.

'My mother was a thrifty woman so I always got the hand-me-downs from my sister. I remember my mother darning socks and repairing clothes, and making marmalade every year, and baking. She was an industrious woman. I remember my mother and auntie saving the wrapping paper at Christmas, they would flatten it out and keep it straight away. She made wonderful parties for the children for our birthdays, and I think I picked that up from her. My mother died when she was fifty, which at the time I thought was old – which is terrible, she was so young! She had been unwell for quite some time, but we thought she would get better.'

Ruth met her future husband while working in catering at a country house in Sussex, where he was a chef, and the pair married in 1986, 'when I was only twenty-two. My mother had passed away in 1984, and it is only now, looking back, that I realise how soon after she died I got married. It didn't feel like two years, it felt like ages. It was such a tough time for our family. My father remarried in the June, and I got married in September, so I had a stepmother and a mother-in-law!'

Their first child, Samuel, was born in 1988, followed by Kirsten in 1991. 'When we first married, we lived with Alan's parents in Bangor in Northern Ireland. Then someone told us about a small cottage to rent on the grounds of Mount Stewart estate, one of the gate lodges. That was where we had Samuel, and we also had dogs and rescue hens. It was idyllic and I loved it, but it was quite isolating too.

'It was around this time that an older Presbyterian minister suggested to Alan that he might have a vocation too. So he decided to try it and studied in Queen's University in Belfast and the Presbyterian College before being appointed as an assistant minister in Fisherwick in Belfast.

'Then he moved to Dublin to the Abbey Presbyterian Church just across from the Garden of Remembrance. When people ask me, I always say, "I don't know what it is like to be married to a minister, I only know what it is like to be married to Alan!" We work as a team, and we work well as a team. A lot of our congregation are from all over the world, it is very international. There are a lot of mums, a lot of single mums, a lot of people I have been able to help. I like to help. I absolutely love children.' This love is reflected in her own career, as a childminder cherished by many Dublin families. Then, when she was only fifty, Ruth became a grandmother when her daughter Kirsten gave birth to Nathan.

> I want my grandchildren to be free
> in themselves, to do the things they
> want to do in life. I would hope
> there is a lot of joy ahead of them.

Ruth says she felt complete in herself when Nathan came along. 'You feel when you become a parent that there is a big adventure ahead of you, but when you become a grandparent, you feel the circle is complete, but in the best possible way.

'My faith is very important to me, and I like to think of it as faith instead of religion. People have an idea of religion as very strict or forced, but for me my faith is much more freeing. It is a way of life, that is fully engaged with what is going on around us, and enjoying life. I would like to see faith in my grandchildren's lives, and I think it is already there, but I would not want them to feel oppressed by the church.

'I want my grandchildren to be free in themselves, to do the things they want to do in life. I would hope there is a lot of joy ahead of them. I think family bonds are very important. I hope, in years to come, my grandchildren will have absorbed all the love and joy and peace and enjoyment in the small things in life. I hope that they will remember me as creative.'

Grandchildren from age seven to five:
Nathan & Abigail

Out from Morning to Night

MARY COUGHLAN

Singer Mary Coughlan was born in Shantalla in Galway in 1956. She recalls playing on the streets there as a child. While her early years at home were often troubled, street life was a place where she thrived.

'I had an extraordinarily happy time on the streets as a child, playing and skipping and skating on the ice. We lived on the street, thrown out from morning to night. We loved it. Kids don't really do that today, it is very different.'

It was a very religious household. 'We were on our knees every evening saying the Rosary and the big scramble would be to see who got the newspaper so we could read the funnies instead! We went to mass on a Sunday, I was very holy. My mother made my beautiful white communion dress and my veil, it was fantastic, she was a great dressmaker but she added a blue ribbon which was very controversial! My sisters and I walked in the May procession every year and my father used to grow peony roses so we'd have flowers to strew in front of the monstrance. I stopped going to mass when I was thirteen.'

Mary's mother also made outfits for good wear for Sunday at the drop of a hat, as well as bridesmaids' dresses for the neighbourhood. 'Later, when I started working at the weekend, I'd see a dress in a magazine and I'd buy a piece of fabric in Galway on a Friday and my mother would help me to make a dress. I'd make a dress almost every weekend and then I'd go to a hop on Saturday night!'

> We were on our knees every
> evening saying the Rosary and the
> big scramble would be to see who got
> the newspaper so we could read the
> funnies instead! We went to mass
> on a Sunday, I was very holy.

Mary also recalls fondly her Donegal grand-mother, Maggie. 'She had red hair, that's where we got the red hair in our family. She was a very strong woman, remarkable. There were very few telephones in Ireland when I was young. She had none and we had none. My father used to put us in the car from time to time to travel up to Burt in Donegal, where she lived. And when we got there, she would have a chicken plucked. She had hens. I swear to God, she would know we were coming. It was the weirdest thing ever, it was the first time I had encountered something like that. She always knew we were coming, it was like telepathy.

'We had great fun there with our cousins in the summer. We fished for tadpoles, we would walk across the fields to the beach; we did very little, but they were good summers. My granny had BBC, because she lived near the border, and I remember seeing *Top of the Pops* for the first time ever! Oh, stop the lights! I listened to Radio Luxembourg and Radio Caroline on a little transistor that I had at home but when we were in Donegal I couldn't believe it. The first band I ever saw were The Honeycombs with 'Have I the Right'. Then there were Procol Harum, The Move with 'Blackberry Way'. It was magic!'

Mary is the eldest in the family but there were joint birthday parties with her younger sister,

Angela, who was eleven months younger than her. 'Mammy also made cakes – she made wedding cakes as well, she was very industrious – we'd have about ten or fifteen in the house for the party.'

I'd buy a piece of fabric in Galway
on a Friday and my mother would help
me to make a dress. I'd make a dress
almost every weekend and then I'd
go to a hop on Saturday night!

There were also gatherings in the house when her father sometimes had Tuesday-night card sessions with neighbours. 'They'd always be playing for a raffle, twenty-fives or something, and all the wives would come and bring sandwiches or the like. The men would be in the kitchen and the women would be in the sitting room and we'd be sitting on the stairs, eavesdropping for any little titbits we could get!'

A couple of weeks after she sat the Leaving Cert, Mary left home. 'I went to Limerick. I knew some people who were from there, and I went to Ennistymon, not really the mecca of runaways! There was a festival on, and I think that's the first time I ever sang in my life. I was singing on the street, and I was invited into a pub to take part in a competition. It was a great experience, great fun. Then I went back to Limerick, and I was working as a waitress in the Galleon Grill. I was there about a week and a very interesting group of people came in, a very big table. They were teachers in the art school in Limerick, and they were talking about how they were using statues for the life drawing classes in the college. They couldn't find anyone to model. So I said, "Well, I'll do it!" I was just seventeen, and it was my first well-paid job, I was getting paid much more than what I was for waitressing.

'I went to London after that, there was a whole heap of people I knew who were moving to London to do this thing called "squatting". I met with a gang of people there from Galway and Limerick and we were squatting in various buildings around London. At this time, I wasn't singing, the only time I had sung was that time in Ennistymon. I sang around the house, but 1984 was the first time I sang in public. I had three children, which was occupying me, and I was trying to make a living, that's what I was concentrating on then.

'I have five children now: Aoife, Olwen, Eoin, Clare and Cian. I was married very young, when

I was nineteen. I had three children first and then split up with my husband in 1984. I went to Dublin to look for a career in the music industry, and I took the three children with me. It was some years later when I met my second husband. I was living in Howth, and I met him there one night, in 1988 or 1989. His name was Frank, he was from LA, and he was just visiting some friends in Howth. We started up a relationship, and he never went back to America after that. He set up his own business here, he invents medical devices. We split up then. I have a partner now, John. I met him in New Zealand.'

Mary's daughter Aoife has two children, Méiní and Luke. 'Méiní is my first grandchild, she is fifteen now. I remember the day she was born so clearly. There were no visitors allowed in the Coombe at the time, so I brought a dressing gown and slippers in the car, and I hung around the doorway of the Coombe and eventually made my way up to the room where Aoife was! No grandparents were allowed in, for some reason. James, Aoife's husband, had been on the phone to me the whole time, telling me what was going on, so I just shoved on the dressing gown and went in the next morning!

'I was a very young granny, but I don't care about that. It was just amazing, it was almost like having another baby. Your baby was having a baby! It was wonderful. I am very close to them all. I got to hold her that first day I went in. I got so excited, I had a cry and I left. It was brilliant.

'I have six grandchildren now. Olwen has Beatrix. Clare, my youngest daughter, has three children, two boys and a girl. My ex-husband was part Italian, and all of the male children in the family were called Felice, so Clare carried on that tradition. The next lad is called Tadhg, he's my man, and Olivia is the little girl. My sons have no children yet.

'I was nervous around overstepping the mark when the grandchildren came along but that was not a problem – I was on call a lot! The whole family were besotted with Méiní when she was born. I have minded them a lot, when the parents needed a night away or anything like that.

'I am blessed with my children. They are extra-ordinarily resourceful, and they are really, really cool kids. They're great role models. When I was Méiní's age, I was always in trouble, I never went to school, but my kids seem to have gotten it right.'

Mary says she is anxious about the future, 'the same as everybody else. And I see it in the kids, that they have anxiety for the future, and the planet, to the extent that some of them have become vegetarian. They love animals too, but they think about the planet a lot. They took part in those climate marches, the school organised it, in 2019. I feel that we have let them down, we've let ourselves down, with the way we have managed our affairs and the planet. That is what I fear. But being optimistic, I think my grandchildren's generation will be the ones who turn it around. It won't be my children, it is too far gone, but it will be *their* children.

'My grandchildren are very wise, but they are very fun as well. We are going on our first proper family holiday this summer, all of us together. I am really looking forward to that. We are very close. I see some of them every day, and some of them stay overnight with me.

> I feel that we have let them down, we've let ourselves down, with the way we have managed our affairs and the planet.

'They know I am a famous singer, they see me on YouTube and that. The little guy is nearly five, and he is completely bewildered by it all. The older ones have been to concerts in Vicar Street. I think it was my sixtieth birthday and they brought a cake out on stage for me, I had no idea they were bringing it out. I brought my granddaughter to the last gig I did in London. She was tickled pink, being brought backstage and all, and how many people were at it.'

But the world her grandchildren inhabit is a very different world from their grandmother's youth. 'I fought very hard. When the family planning clinic in Galway was set up originally, I was giving out information to women about it. My grandchildren don't have to think about stuff like that now, they have other things to think about. But we fought for abortion, contraception, divorce, same-sex marriage – and we got it.

'My grandchildren are not old enough to be thinking about all of that, but they have far bigger things that they are thinking about. Hunger, peace, the planet – that is what a lot of them are concerned about. They have huge respect for animals and the planet. Which is not something I would have thought about at their age!'

And how would Mary like to be remembered by her grandchildren? 'As someone who is great craic, but they think that anyway! I don't like thinking about them remembering me. We live up here in the foothills of the Wicklow mountains, it is a great, safe place and they come here a lot.

'I have planning permission to build an extension on to the side of my house now, and my youngest daughter Clare and her husband and the kids are moving in. Clare grows everything that we eat for the summer, her gardening skills are legendary! We have hens as well. I would love to have the whole family up here. We all get on so well together. It is something I am eternally grateful for. We are never far away from each other.

'I wrote a song on my last album for my grandchildren, it is called "Safe and Sound". I have no wisdom to pass onto them, they are wiser than I am.'

Always know you're safe and sound at home
I will keep you safe and homeward bound.

From 'Safe and Sound' from the album *Life Stories* (2020)

Grandchildren from age fifteen to one:
Méiní, Luke, Felice, Beatrix, Tadhg & Olivia

The Parcel from America

BRÍD MARTIN

Growing up in Rossaveal in Connemara, Bríd Martin was the fifth born of ten children, five boys and five girls. She remembers happy, communal living, in a home where her mother made a lot of their clothes. The 'parcels from America' have a special place in reminiscence – their cousins would receive them from relatives there, and eventually Bríd and her siblings got to enjoy the hand-me-downs.

She recalls being spoiled by her older sisters when they began working, and the special occasion of a trip to Galway city, where she got to choose her own shop-bought dress – a big novelty!

Early memories are punctuated by the social gatherings, and these happened far and wide. 'Lots of people had hooleys, for any and every occasion! All twelve of us used to go to them, there were always sing-songs and music. My mother was very musical and we lived next door to the pub so we always had partying and merriment.'

This love of music was encouraged in primary school in Rossaveal where Bríd recalls a 'marvellous teacher', Tadhg O'Shea. 'He was a bit of a genius. He had translated all the Christmas carols from France and Holland and Spain, and put them into a booklet, and we would be singing them to our hearts' content in the school.'

She also has vivid memories of the economics of her first holy communion, and the largesse she received from one grandmother – a half a crown, 'a fortune then!' It was a religious household; the family knelt to pray every evening. 'We'd each say a decade [of the Rosary] but we'd be sniggering as well! Oh God, we used to be killed for laughing! Even now we have a laugh at what we were like as children.'

However, there were favourite saints. 'If we lost something, we always prayed to St Anthony. And I used to pray at the statue of Our Lady in the church whenever we had exams. Then we were marched up to confessions on Christmas Eve. My poor mother used to go too and all the work she had done, as if she had ever done anything wrong! But we'd come home from midnight mass and we'd see all the lights of Carraroe and the candles lighting in the windows. It was magic really.'

Lots of people had hooleys, for any and every occasion! All twelve of us used to go to them, there were always sing-songs and music. My mother was very musical and we lived next door to the pub so we always had partying and merriment!

The family also had great devotion to Knock. 'My mother, Mary, went to Knock regularly with her mother, Mary Nee.' Bríd still visits Knock and brings home bottles of holy water. She laughs as she recalls her own grandson commenting on this in recent times, and how the priest said it isn't to be used because of Covid-19! She still believes in the power of holy water, and its protective effects. 'The *uisce na Cincíse*, Ascension Day, was very important.'

She recalls the art of storytelling and bemoans its disappearance and the over-reliance today on the distractions of phones and iPads. 'When we were young there was a neighbour down the road, Coílín Jonnie, and he'd come in every night and we'd all be waiting for him. We'd sit around him and he'd continue with whatever story he was telling us. And we played games; one of our favourites was *Lubabhán larabhán*, where we'd sit around in a circle and put our foot inside until we had two feet in and we were safe.'

We'd come home from midnight
mass and we'd see all the lights of
Carraroe and the candles lighting
in the windows. It was magic really.

Bríd recalls how traditions were passed on, such as bread- and boxty-making, or the crafts of knitting and weaving. 'I saw all of that. I saw the sheep being shorn and the wool being woven. We had to do everything, and in doing so, we learned everything. I was able to make white sauce and wash the socks, and I knew wool shouldn't go into really hot water and all that … I don't think that happens now.' She also recalls how nothing was wasted, as even the skin of potatoes was given to the donkeys.

Bríd went on to study home economics in college and then taught the children of the army personnel in the Curragh camp. But adventure beckoned and she joined Voluntary Services Overseas (VSO) and was sent to Uganda in east Africa, where she worked with the Sacred Heart nuns, teaching nutrition and sewing, before returning to Ireland.

Back in Galway she took a job in the Hotel Training College in Athenry and soon met her future husband at a disco in Mullingar. Socialising centred on the dance halls and discos and the cinema in Galway. 'Cinema was a big thing and we had marvellous films.'

The couple went on to have four children, three of whom survive. 'My second child, Catherine, lived for five months but she had a heart issue. We were going to bring her to Great Ormond Street for a transplant, but sadly she didn't make it.'

When her family was young, they lived in a 'special' home in Sligo, the house where Irish-language scholar Douglas Hyde spent the first seven years of his life.

Today she is the proud grandmother of five. Her first, Christian, was born nineteen years ago, the day before Bríd's own mother, Mary McDonagh, died. She laments the fact that she never told her mother that Patrick and his girlfriend Louise were expecting, fearing that a woman of her generation would judge a baby born out of wedlock. She feels that nonetheless her mother may have picked up that there was news on the horizon, and hopes this is so.

> I saw the sheep being shorn and the wool being woven. We had to do everything, and in doing so, we learned everything. I was able to make white sauce and wash the socks, and I knew wool shouldn't go into really hot water.

By this time, Bríd was principal of Coola post-primary school and she recalls the joy of first meeting Christian, and watching each stage, including his first steps. 'We had more time with him than we had with our own children!'

And what does she wish for the upcoming generation? 'I would love my grandchildren to get into whatever field they want to get into. I would want them to be able to stand on their own two feet, and speak up for whatever they believe in.

'I learned a lot from the people in my life. I'm

not sure how I would like to be remembered by my grandchildren – hopefully as someone who was always willing to lend a listening ear, but I can say that they probably will remember me as a very hard teacher who made them learn Irish!'

Grandchildren from age nineteen to five:
Christian, Donncha, Aodháin, Iona & Noínín

Chasing the Bread Van

MARTIN SWORDS

Martin documented his own childhood story in his book *Tea in the Burlington: A Memoir*, which tells how he discovered, at the age of thirty-eight, that his unmarried aunt, Kathleen, was actually his birth mother. It was an informal family adoption by Kathleen's brother, Pat, and his wife, Mary. 'There was no adoption legislation in those days, many families around had children who were born to somebody, and the family took it and reared it and it was all grand.'

Martin recalls the day when Kathleen told him her secret. 'Myself and my wife, Jacinta, were having a cup of tea in the Burlington with Kathleen, who was in a Donnybrook nursing home at the time. We were always a family who were interested in old times and stories. I had no suspicions at all, about anything. I said to Kathleen, "Tell me about May and Pat before I was born in 1950," thinking I was born to May. Being an only child, I asked if May had problems, a hysterectomy or anything, could she not have any more children? And Kathleen said, "Well, actually, May didn't have any children. *I* had the child, and you *are* the child." We were stunned.

'I describe it as my "drowning man moment", because everything explained itself in an instant. Why Kathleen was always around ... we all have aunts, but this was a special aunt, who was always there, and part and parcel of my upbringing. She lived with May and Pat a lot, and was a great hand in my education, she probably paid for most of it actually.'

There was no adoption legislation
in those days, many families around
had children who were born to
somebody, and the family took it
and reared it and it was all grand.

It was only after Martin learned of this that he realised how difficult it must have been for Kathleen, although he also recognises that there was a certain joy there too. 'She was living with her son … well, not her son. And then if you look at it from May's point of view, she is rearing her son who isn't really her son, and the natural mother is living under the same roof. It was a common practice when I was a child, there is less confusion for today's children in terms of knowing who they are.'

The thinking around baptism has also changed since Martin was young. 'When I was born in Holles Street, it was the practice to get the child baptised as soon as possible, the nurse used to take the baby out and down to Westland Row. Today many families wait months before the child is baptised.

'I have great memories of the very simple life we led as children in the fifties, growing up in Dún Laoghaire. We played outside on the street with the other lads. You'd be playing football or robbing apples or "scutting" along behind the Johnston Mooney & O'Brien bread van.' Martin refers here to the popular kids' game of jumping onto the ledge on the back of a van as it moved off. 'When I was four or five I tore the legs off myself doing that. I was dragged along behind it for a bit, my knees were in ribbons. I was showered with love then and lathered in calamine lotion and I had a bandage a young boy would be proud of! I was reading at an early age because I was encouraged by Kathleen to take out books from the library. I was an only child – with two mothers and a da!

It was the practice to get the child baptised as soon as possible, the nurse used to take the baby out and down to Westland Row. Today many families wait months before the child is baptised.

'Parties were rare but great, often in honour of a visiting relation from America. Hectic reshuffling of furniture, chairs up on beds, and rugs rolled up to make room for music and dancing. Nights often ended with Uncle John standing by the fire, hand on the mantelpiece holding a Jameson, giving us "I'll take you home again, Kathleen", his standby song. We children listened from the bend in the stairs, way past our bedtime.'

Martin also remembers the prevalence of holy water at the time. 'Holy water was everywhere, and always in the little font just inside the front door; it often had a little sponge in it to prevent the water from drying up. You blessed yourself every time you left the house, and you were asked and reminded to do it. At Easter you were sent down to the church to get a large bottle of the newly blessed fresh holy water for future use.'

Martin met his wife, Jacinta, when he was fifteen years old. 'It was kind of love at first sight, she was going to Cluny secondary school in Killiney, and if I was free I went up and stood outside the gate and carried her books.' The pair are now forty-eight years married and Martin recalls their engagement, there was no getting down on one knee with a ring or anything like that. 'I remember we were at home in her parents' house having a chat, and saying, "I suppose we will get married then?"'

One of Martin's most vivid memories is the birth of his second son, Mark, in Holles Street hospital. 'I had to drive Jacinta in that morning in a clapped-out Fiat that I had bought from a fella I worked with for next to nothing, and it wouldn't start! It was snowing. We arrived in to Holles Street, in February 1978. The eighth of February. I arrived at the top of Holles Street, I could see the hospital in front of me and the car wouldn't go, so Jacinta and I had to get out and push the car into the kerb! She was barely up the stairs when the baby was born.'

When David and Mark were born, their grand-parents were around, but they weren't as hands-on as today's grandparents. 'They were older and wiser, and we were younger and thought we knew everything. But of course the old fogies had plenty of wisdom! We got advice from them, and we listened and took it.

'Our first grandchild was Sean Mark Swords, son of David and Fiona. He was born early, at twenty-six weeks, and we couldn't hold him for a while because he was in an incubator, but we used to visit all the time and just look in at him and pray that he would get through, and he did. He was a fighter! He is twelve now.'

David has Sean and Mark has Julian (seven) and Charlotte (two), the first girl! 'It was so terrific to meet her. We weren't allowed to go in and see her because it was in the middle of Covid. We finally got to see her when she was about a fortnight old. When she was born, to my great surprise, with no encouragement from me or Jacinta or anybody, they named her Charlotte Kathleen Swords, which we were delighted about.

'Increasingly now, young parents are living far away, in Australia and New Zealand, and Mammy and Daddy can Zoom with their children and grandchildren all they like but it is really not the same. And the other thing that is worth remarking on is – where children fall out with their parents, the grandchildren are being used as a threat. You know, "Well, that's fine, but we won't be visiting with the grandchildren."'

> We played outside on the street with the other lads. You'd be playing football or robbing apples or 'scutting' along behind the Johnston Mooney & O'Brien bread van.

Jacinta joins us then to say that all she wants for their grandchildren is 'to be happy, and safe. I feel for them, and I think it is hard for them. It is harder than when we were growing up. We were less pressured. These days there are more distractions and with more distractions comes more danger.'

Martin says he sees a difference between grandad and the grandchildren, and grandma and the grandchildren. 'I will take them out in the garden and turn over stones and point out little wriggly things. Do more practical stuff with them. We had Charlotte here in the garden in a little teepee thing made out of bamboo sticks and a cloth and clothes pegs, the easiest thing in the world to make – she has knocked more craic out of that. She gets in, she takes the teddies and the dollies and puts them to bed in the little tent. Hours and hours of craic. Jacinta will involve them in a different way, in cooking and baking.'

'We make a big mess,' Jacinta says, 'pull the stool over and put the child up and give him a little spoon and a bowl of water and let them off and they love it! We would take out saucepans and wooden spoons and they would knock hours of entertainment out of that. The child is delighted and stirring away and there is a simplicity in that that works really well.'

Martin and Jacinta's youngest grandchild was born during lockdown, and Martin wrote this poem for her.

My Charlotte

You are greatly loved and welcome.
Arriving in the lockdown, you will not be
Restrained or hemmed in.
The wide world will be your playground,
All of nature your school.
You will be guided in the lessons of life.
You will learn soon that a smile, a grin, a laugh,
A twinkle of eyes can melt the hearts of family,
Of grandparents, and especially of grannies.

Soon you will know the power you have
With a girly grin, a sweet smile, a giggle.
Your brother Julian may fish for crabs
But you will love the elegant grace of swans.
Held close and protected in your warm
And loving family
Know that you are for us
My Charlotte, our Charlotte,
Charlotte

Grandchildren from age twelve to two:
Sean, Julian & Charlotte

Bread Baking on the Open Fire

MARY ROSE MURPHY

Self-sufficiency was the order of the day for Mary Rose Murphy's family growing up on the Howth Road in Blackbanks, Raheny in the fifties. 'We had a big garden and we kept hens and chickens and grew our own vegetables. We had a big range in the kitchen so the fire was always on and it was around the hearth, it was warm and secure. It was a very hospitable home because our parents, relations and friends and our cousins would come and our own friends would be in so it was a very full house.

'We had great fun and freedom growing up. Our parents could put their hands to anything – and were skilled cooks, gardeners, dressmakers and knitters.

I have a lovely memory of my mother's friends gathering in the evening around the fire to do their darning together and they had great chats. Everybody knew the stories of each other's backgrounds and families. The stories of a generation are carried and told by the women.

We had a big garden and we kept
hens and chickens and grew our own
vegetables. We had a bigrange in
the kitchen so the fire was always
on and it was around the hearth,
it was warm and secure.

'And there wasn't any waste. When I look back to my grandparents and my great-grandparents I see how very resourceful they were, how self-reliant. They made their own clothes, everything was used and reused and I think that was a tremendous thing. I would just like if future generations could have that resourcefulness but also the strength of character of knowing that they are resilient, strong people, I think that is hugely important. That stood to me personally through my life, knowing that I am descended from a lot of strong, resilient people, and

I would want to pass that strength and knowledge on to future generations. We all had so many jobs and household chores to do when we were growing up. We were never allowed out to play until the work was done.

'To entertain ourselves, there were musical evenings and a lot of big parties or hooleys in the house, big family parties when all the cousins and all the relations would come. My parents held musical evenings, there were a lot of very good singers, especially in my father's house. One of his brothers in particular, he was a priest, and he had a marvellous tenor voice.

'Then every St Stephen's Day, my mother would invite the Murphy relations. There were huge amounts of food. My mother was a great caterer, a tremendous baker of cakes, there was a great lavishness about it all. I absolutely loved it. My father's relations were all from around Dublin but then my mother's were all from the country and when they came they would stay, so that would be a different type of catering because it would be less lavish and more prolonged. You would be thrown out of your bed or somebody else would be in your bed, so you would be very squashed! It was a four-bedroom house and the only person in the house with their own room was Rita, who was our live-in maid. My children find that hilarious, but we were squashed enough really because there was seldom a time when people weren't actually staying and sometimes people would come for long periods of time – it was a full house.

'On my mother's side of the family, my grand-mother lived in Roscommon. She died when I was quite young but I have a very fond memory of her grasping my young hands in her work-worn elderly hands and smiling at me. She was a very productive farmer's wife and I have lovely memories of visiting her and the smell of turf and bread baking on the open fire and the big dresser in her kitchen full of lovely big plates.

'As a child there was a fair bit of running around and football with the brothers, and chasing. Now, because we lived on a main road as such, I used to envy people who lived in housing estates because they could go out and play on the road! We also played "Queenie-eye-o, who has the ball?"'

Mary Rose met her husband, John, when she accompanied a friend to a disco. 'I didn't particularly want to go, it was my friend who wanted to meet the man – who I subsequently married – on the bus on the way into town!'

Married in 1973, the couple had three daughters. Mary Rose then trained as a marriage guidance counsellor with Accord, and eleven years later did Women's Studies in UCD.

> I have a lovely memory of my mother's friends gathering in the evening around the fire to do their darning together and they had great chats. Everybody knew the stories of each other's backgrounds and families. The stories of a generation are carried and told by the women.

They now have four grandchildren, two boys and two girls aged from 8 to 18. Mary Rose remembers the day her first grandchild was born. 'He was a tiny little person, he had to be delivered about a month early so he was only about four pounds and he needed a lot of care. I found it difficult to understand how somebody could write themselves into your heart so quickly. Absolutely imprinted on me. I mean when you have your children you love them greatly but this is a whole different level of experience and it happened with each of the grandchildren. My grandchildren love the way we are so fit and active, and we have a very good joking type of relationship with them.'

But there's another side to Mary Rose. Her Spanish great-grandmother, Amelia Connor (née Capacete) and her daughter Elizabeth Murphy (née Connor), are believed to have been the inspirations for Molly Bloom in James Joyce's *Ulysses*.

Mary Rose's great-grandfather Bernard Connor, who was born in Ireland, joined the British army and was shipped off to Gibraltar, where he fell in love with and married Amelia Capacete. In *Ulysses*, Molly Bloom is an opera singer from Gibraltar. She is the daughter of Sergeant Major Brian Tweedy.

> My parents held musical evenings,
> there were a lot of very good singers,
> especially in my father's house. One of
> his brothers in particular, he was a priest,
> and he had a marvellous tenor voice.

In 1904, the summer in which *Ulysses* was set, the seeds of it were taking root in Joyce's mind, and Bernard and Amelia were living with their daughter Elizabeth on North Strand in Dublin, around the corner from James Joyce, and just ten doors up from the home of his favourite aunt, Josephine Murray. Joyce stayed with Josephine during that summer. The parallels in the circumstances of the real and fictional lives are uncanny.

Mary Rose says, 'Amelia Connor (née Capacete) and her daughter Elizabeth Murphy (née Connor) have always been somewhat exotic figures in the Murphy family. Elizabeth and her husband, William, were beautiful singers and met in a musical society. Her family always spoke with great pride about their half-Spanish mother. The next generation of Murphys, now in their sixties and seventies, had no idea until recently of the connection.

'The only one of that family I actually met was Great-Uncle Fred Connor, who was a chaplain to the Royal Irish Fusiliers in Gallipoli. He stored a lot of his paraphernalia in our attic on the Howth Road. I particularly remember the fun we had playing in the back garden in the tent he used in Gallipoli and also a stretcher from the battlefield.'

Grandchildren from age eighteen to eight:
Killian, Enda, Caoimhe & Neassa.

The Guards
Mowed the Grass

PETER GORDON

Peter Gordon was born in 1936, on the day the
Spanish Civil War broke out. The father of five
and grandfather of eleven is from Mohill, County
Leitrim and moved to Dublin as a young man. He
had a long career in retail, running his own grocery
shop, 'Pete's Place', in Crumlin for over twenty
years. His late wife Olive was a teacher. Peter's own
career began when his mother refused to allow him
join the British army: 'In those days boys did what
their mothers told them.' So instead he joined the
then Allied Dublin Merchants, which morphed into
the Londis group.

Peter remembers growing up in Mohill, a town

of only 750 residents at the time. 'Everybody knew everybody else. The local gardaí, to kill time, mowed the grass around the garda station. As there was no crime, hall doors were never locked. The only offences then were having no light on your bicycle or after-hours drinking in the pubs.

'We played on the streets from morning to night during holiday time. We left the house around nine o'clock and only returned to get a slice of bread and jam to keep the energy levels topped up. In the 1940s and 1950s Mohill was the leading business town in the midlands and west of Ireland. People came there for all their big purchases. The place where I worked had a staff of thirty-six. There were twenty-seven pubs, five garages, two bakeries, three butcher shops and five forges, all thriving.

Everybody knew everybody else.
The local gardaí, to kill time, mowed
the grass around the garda station.
As there was no crime, hall doors were
never locked. The only offences then
were having no light on your bicycle or
after-hours drinking in the pubs.

'By the end of the 1960s, the town had gone into decline. It had been supported locally by a thriving farming community who fed hundreds of pigs, hens and cattle. The younger generation decided that this kind of hardship was not for them so they either emigrated or went to college. Instead of the shovel, they decided to use the laptop.

> Rationing had been introduced and we were given ration books with coupons. Each person was allowed one ounce of tea, one ounce of butter, a small amount of soap and an ounce of sugar per week.

'We had a great social life and on Sunday nights we went to the Cloudland Ballroom in Rooskey for the dancing. All the top Irish showbands played there. Sometimes there would be an English band on stage such as Acker Bilk or Kenny Ball. Another great band that folded in the late 1960s was the Savoy Swing Seven from Carrick-on-Shannon. At one stage I put myself forward to manage them, but Albert Reynolds got the job. Albert and his brother Jim owned fifteen big dance halls around Ireland so the band members figured that they would get plenty of bookings through Albert. It was a case of what might have been!'

Peter was only a small child when the Second World War broke out but he remembers the later years when there was a scarcity of food in Ireland. 'Rationing had been introduced and we were given ration books with coupons. Each person was allowed one ounce of tea, one ounce of butter, a small amount of soap and an ounce of sugar per week. By the time the war finished, I was nine years old.'

But as Britain took a battering during the war, many Irish people went there to work. 'The wages were much better in the UK than in Ireland. Most of my brothers and sisters went too, working in nursing, the civil service, teaching, engineering and the diplomatic corps. At Christmas, many of the people who had gone to London for work returned home for the holiday. I do not know if my memory is playing tricks on me or not but the young men all seemed to be wearing black suits and white shirts. They all seemed to have black hair well styled with hair oil. Britain appeared to be suiting them very well as they seemed to have plenty of money to spare. It is well known that these men sent money home every week to help their parents, so much so that an amount was mentioned on the annual government budget as "Remittances from emigrants".'

There were parties and hooleys when the emigrants came home in the fifties, and much of the celebrations centred around Mohill's twenty-seven pubs. 'On Saturday nights the pubs had live music – accordions, fiddles and flutes were played by really good local musicians and there were local ballad singers, two of whom had won All-Ireland ballad contests, so the standard was high.'

Peter met his wife, Olive, at a dance in Palmerstown Rugby Club and they got married nine months afterwards and had five children. The eldest grandchild is thirteen-year-old Emma and Peter remembers the excitement of the day he met her for the first time. 'She was small enough to hold in one hand, and now she is a big girl in secondary school.'

The wages were much better in the UK than in Ireland. Most of my brothers and sisters went too, working in nursing, the civil service, teaching, engineering and the diplomatic corps. At Christmas, many of the people who had gone to London for work returned home for the holiday.

Peter believes in the importance of praising your children and grandchildren, recalling earlier times when such things were frowned upon. He hopes his grandchildren will grow up to be good people. 'Grandparents are important people in the lives of their grandchildren, they all have big hugs for me when they see me. I don't think they have a harder life than we had but they have more challenges now with housing and all that kind of thing. But that hasn't affected them yet, they haven't encountered anything drastic yet.'

He would like to be remembered as 'somebody that was funny and caring, I think that would be a good legacy'.

Peter's legacy also includes twenty years of writing for the *Leitrim Guardian* and of taking priests to task for the length of their sermons. 'I was a shopkeeper and I used to go to mass on a Saturday evening so that I would be able to open on Sunday, but one of the priests, he actually could put me to sleep. I used to time his sermons, about fifteen minutes each time, and I wrote to the archbishop about it. One of the secretaries wrote back and said thank you for my letter and he must pass it on to the man who teaches the young priests. Of course, that was the big mistake because it was not the young priests that were causing the trouble, it was the old fellas!'

Peter believes that when he arrives at the gates of heaven, the fact that he worked as a shopkeeper for so many years and followed the Leitrim Gaelic football team will influence St Peter, who'll say, 'Come in here immediately, you've suffered enough!'

Grandchildren from age thirteen to one:
Emma, Rachel, Juliette, Oliver, Sebastian, Anna,
Isabel, Hugh, Alex, James & Daniel

The Rector's Daughter

RUTH BUCHANAN

Ruth Buchanan grew up in the parish of Carbury in County Kildare in the 1950s, where her father was a Church of Ireland clergyman. She has very happy memories of an 'idyllic' childhood. 'We were living in the most beautiful Georgian rectory you ever saw in your life. One of my earliest memories is as a toddler playing outside the house. There was a grassy slope and I was playing with an egg cup, and it rolled down and I couldn't get it. I would have been about three years old then.

'Another memory from Carbury was that a monkey used to come into my bedroom, at least I believed it was a monkey, and it really upset me. My father got out his paintbrush and painted the shutters, where the monkey was, and I never saw it again – he painted away the monkey!

'When I was four or five, we moved to what I call my hometown, Mountmellick in County Laois. It was a very Protestant town. There was a Presbyterian church, a Methodist church, a Church of Ireland, and of course a Catholic church. It was very much a Quaker town, famous for its embroidery in the early nineteenth century. My father had two parishes initially, Mountmellick and Coolbanagher, but Rosenallis and Clonaslee were added later on so he was a busy man.

'Our house, the rectory, was in the square, facing one of the bigger shops, Pim's. Not far away was a wonderful bakery, Sheil's, and there was also a butcher. Wattie Walsh ran the chemist on the corner and also acted as vet to our many dogs, cats and rabbit. The street to the right of the square led to the post office, McEvoy's shop and the dentist. Those of us who had teeth filled will never forget the dentist. He had his main practice in Portlaoise, then called Maryborough. We all preferred to be treated in Portlaoise because in that surgery he had an electric drill. In his Mountmellick surgery his drill was worked by his foot! It was a pedal drill and took forever. Not only that but he did not approve of injections for children! However, my own teeth are still in pretty good condition and I'm sure his pedal drill has contributed to that. Also on that street was the Presentation Convent where Miss Foley taught me piano. It was quite unusual for Protestants to visit convents at the time and I was a bit uncomfortable being surrounded by nuns in habits but they were very kind and Miss Foley was the perfect piano teacher for a tiny beginner.

Mountmellick in County Laois ... was
a very Protestant town. There was a
Presbyterian church, a Methodist church,
a Church of Ireland, and of course a
Catholic church. It was very much a
Quaker town, famous for its embroidery
in the early nineteenth century.

'The street to the left of our house led to the two banks in the town, Shaw's shops and the parish priest's house and it was outside that house that I first set eyes on Éamon de Valera though I had no idea who he was at the time. I was passing the priest's house when I noticed a crowd of camera men and reporters ... I didn't know what they were at the time either! I was held back for what seemed like a long time while they took pictures and talked to him. I was not impressed and was quite surprised when that same man became Uachtarán na hÉireann!

'The Protestant school was very close to the home of Oliver J. Flanagan, our local Fine Gael TD who looked after his local constituents very well and was rewarded at each election. To get to it from The Square we had to walk down a narrow road where Denny's pig factory was situated. Pigs from all over the place were brought there to be slaughtered. And they knew what was going to happen. I can still hear the squeals of the poor creatures when they were herded from the lorry to their deaths.

'Mountmellick boasts a river and a canal, a branch of the Grand Canal from former times. The Slieve Bloom mountains are also nearby so, as children, we spent a lot of time outside. We caught pinkeens in the Owenass river, a tributary of The Barrow. We rode our bikes up the mountains and swam in quite dangerous waters unknown to our parents. And we all survived. It was the days of "Go out and play", and we did. As long as we were home by six o'clock, nobody worried.

'I think it is very different for children now.

I would be much more protective of my grand-children than my mother would have been of me. There was nothing to be afraid of then, and maybe there still isn't but people are much more wary.

'Our Christmases revolved around Christianity and the birth of Jesus. Our own family Christmas was always a bit spoiled because Daddy was off doing services in three or four parishes, and we always had to have everything very late. Easter was a special time too. Good Friday was very serious when I was a child. I always thought the fact that Jesus was crucified was dreadfully depressing. We were marched off to prayers in the church. There was a general confession, you didn't have to confess anything individually.

We caught pinkeens in the Owenass
river, a tributary of The Barrow.
We rode our bikes up the mountains
and swam in quite dangerous waters
unknown to our parents.

'I was always conscious that my father was the rector, especially when I got to my teenage years. Mountmellick was an ecumenical town, people mixed very well. I remember being invited to the National Bank manager's son's party, it was a Saturday night. We had to leave at midnight because it was the Sabbath and I was mortified, as nobody else was leaving.

'I was a boarder in the Collegiate school in Celbridge, which was basically a school for poor Protestants at the time. It closed down and became part of Kilkenny College. English was my favourite subject, we had the most wonderful English teacher. She used to bring us to the theatre and spend her own money bringing us places and educating us.

'Then there were the parties back in Mount-mellick. This is where the ecumenism sort of died though, because they were purely Protestant affairs. No Catholics were allowed in. I remember visiting the town years later, in the seventies, and I met the rector there, whom I'd known in Trinity. He was showing me round the town again, and we were in the hall and I said, "I presume it's mixed now?" and he said, "Oh no …!" Things were slow to change in that regard.

'Both of our children married Catholics, and our in-laws couldn't be nicer. We are extremely close to each of our six grandchildren, every one is a miracle. When you become a granny, it takes a little while for you to realise you've actually attained that status! I was fifty-something when our first grandchild Tom was born. The first is special as it turns you into a grandmother.

'We have been pretty hands-on, as grandparents. We live a distance away, which is a good thing because my husband Shane would be gnawing at the door to see them if we were next door. He is a doting grandfather, he worships the ground they walk on. We both do.

'For my part, I feed them. Each of them has a favourite pudding. Tom's is brownies. Sarah is the easiest, she will eat anything. Millie is very difficult and likes ginger in things. Ed likes apple tart. Issy likes meringues, and Eve likes everything! All of them grew up in Dublin and I often think it would have been nice for them to have had the experience of growing up in a small town like I did. But, then again, I couldn't wait to get out of Mountmellick when I was seventeen!

'If I was asked to give advice to my grand-children, I would tell them to enjoy themselves, to try and be happy, and that everything awful passes eventually. I think this generation's children are much more aware of life than I was. They have a lot more serious issues to deal with than us. We didn't know anything about climate change. It was easier to believe in a religion, there were real jobs that people had for life. That isn't happening anymore.

'But if a lot more is expected of children at an early age today, they are also better equipped than we were and know so much more about life. At school, they have a better experience than my generation. Hitting children was tolerated in my day, thankfully that's changed now.

> Our own family Christmas was always a bit spoiled because Daddy was off doing services in three or four parishes, and we always had to have everything very late. Easter was a special time too. Good Friday was very serious when I was a child.

'Unlike my childhood, religion plays no big part in the lives of my grandchildren. That doesn't bother me in the slightest. I still love going to church because I love the Protestant hymns, but I am afraid religion doesn't play a big part in my own life anymore. A friend put up a picture on Facebook of a starving baby and asked, "What good God would let a baby die like this?" You do wonder, don't you?

'I love the idea of a God, and I love the Christian story – in many ways, it gave us limits, which can be good. It gave a form to the week, Sunday was special. We didn't do much on Sundays. Daddy was working, of course. It was a quiet day, a family day. That has gone, in a way. People aren't getting married in churches as much these days. They're not getting married at all, it doesn't matter anymore. I think that's good, that people don't feel obliged to get married if they don't want to. But they can have a baby if they want to.

'In terms of the values that I would want to pass down to my grandchildren, that would be caring for people and the world around them. My husband Shane Ross was involved in politics, and I would perhaps encourage my grandchildren to join organisations that help people who need it, because there are so many people that need help. We need to look after each other now more than ever. And I can't think of better young people to make a contribution than our wonderful six grandchildren.'

Grandchildren from age twenty-three to eight:
Tom, Sarah, Millie, Ed, Issy & Eve

A Babushka of Ukraine

MARINA SEVRINA

In 2022, Ireland welcomed over 40,000 Ukrainian people into the country, including hundreds of 'babushkas', or grandmothers, and their families, who sought refuge here on fleeing the war in their homeland.

I spoke to one such grandmother, Marina Sevrina, who is now living in group accommodation at Coolnagreina in Greystones in County Wicklow, with her daughter and grandchildren. They are one of twenty-four families there, including a number of children who are now enrolled in the local school.

Marina recalls her childhood, growing up in western Ukraine, as very happy. 'I loved school, I was very musical, my favourite band was ABBA. I love classical music as well and I went to a music school and I became a teacher of piano.

'I worked as a piano teacher for a few years, and after that I joined the military and played the drums in the military orchestra and I was a soldier. I am retired from the military now.

'My mother and father were wonderful parents. Every year we would go to Odessa for a holiday, to swim in the sea. We lived in our country house during the summer. Every year, me and my husband and my daughters go to the dacha, and we have our own little farm and harvest berries.

'In Ireland, when you go to your summer houses, you relax and have green grass and flowers but, in our summer houses, we have orchards and apple trees and vegetables growing and we have to work! We harvest it all and eat it over the winter.'

Brother and sister Timotey and Nastya, who are also staying in Greystones, join us with their own memories of childhood in Ukraine. 'Remember the family holidays by the sea? We drove by car for a long time, it was really hot. We stayed in a tent and there were beautiful sunsets. As kids we swam and caught jellyfish,' says Timotey.

Fishing was another favourite pastime and whole families would head to the sea to fish for Black Sea bass. 'We would fry it and eat it but sometimes we wouldn't catch anything for an hour or so.'

Winter was also a wonderful time for children, with heavy snowfalls. 'We have a lot of snow and every year we went sledding,' says Nastya. 'We also played snowballs on the way home from school. It was a carefree time with no talk of any war.'

The young Marina met her husband in military college. 'He was the conductor of the orchestra. It was love at first sight! We got married in 1983, and we had two girls, Anastasia and Olesya. Anastasia has two sons, Max is three and Danny is one. Olesya has one son, Oleg, who is fifteen. Anastasia is here in Ireland with Max and Danny, and Olesya also fled from the war and is living in Luxembourg. Their partners are still in Ukraine. It is very sad.'

Marina remembers the moment she met her first grandchild, Oleg. 'I was a young babushka. I was very emotional. When I held him in my arms, I felt he was part of me, part of myself. I have a very close relationship with my grandchildren. I love them very much and I am a good babushka!'

> I was a young babushka. I was very
> emotional. When I held him in my arms,
> I felt he was part of me, part of myself.

On coming to Ireland, Marina says she and her family feel 'so lucky to be alive!' They were on a family holiday in the Carpathian mountains when the first Russian rockets started to hit Ukraine. 'On the first day of war, it was me, my daughter and her husband and mother-in-law, and the grandchildren. When the Russian attacks started, we realised that the only sensible thing to do was to leave as quickly as possible. We live in Kyiv, but we never went back home. We left the mountains and drove straight to Poland. We didn't go back, we didn't collect anything, we just left everything behind. We were all in my daughter, Anastasia's car. Her husband was with us, but we had to say goodbye to him and left him in Ukraine.

'It was a long trip in the car, with military planes flying very low over us. We were terrified. The children didn't know what was happening, they had come from a normal, happy family holiday to this! There were hundreds of families trying to escape in their cars, the roads were full, everyone was trying to run away.

'We got to the Polish border and crossed there and met with Polish volunteers who were helping people trying to get out of Ukraine. We only had our holiday clothes. A little bag, nothing else. We stayed in a hotel for a few days, trying to decide where to go next and then we decided to move to Ireland. Friends told us that it was a good place to go and we knew a little because we had been taught about it in school, about the conflict with England. We identified with that, so we thought Ireland would be a good place to come.'

I want my grandchildren to live in peace, and grow up to be happy and kind and good people. Intelligent and thoughtful.

They arrived in Dublin in March 2022. 'We came here to Coolnagreina that first night. We were very frightened and worried. When we arrived, one of my grandchildren was very sick with a stomach bug. Everybody had it in Poland, and when we got here, a doctor in the airport got an ambulance for him and he was treated in hospital. But he is well again now, I think it was caused by stress.'

The peaceful atmosphere in their Wicklow accommodation belies the horror and chaos that Marina and the rest of the women and children have left behind them. They occupy themselves by cooking and caring for the children and keeping up with news from Ukraine. They sit in the gardens drinking tea and smoking, playing football with the kids and listening to the news and wondering when they will be able to return to Ukraine and resume their lives.

'We miss Ukraine terribly. In Kyiv our house is still safe and intact at the moment. We watch the news every day and see the damage to the city. A lot of people have left, it is almost empty. We stay in touch with people from Kyiv to make sure they are okay and they keep us up to date on our friends and tell us our house is still standing.

'We have no idea how long we are going to be in Ireland, but we hope that the war finishes soon so we can go back home. I don't want to find a house here in Ireland because I want to go home, but I do want to find a job. I have very bad English though, so I can't teach. I am trying my best to learn.

'I want my grandchildren to live in peace, and grow up to be happy and kind and good people. Intelligent and thoughtful. I want them to be able to live in Ukraine. I don't want them to have to deal with war.'

Grandchildren from age fifteen to one:
Oleg, Max & Danny

Transporting a
Coffin on a Sleigh

TOM MCGRATH

Tom McGrath laments the fact that children today don't have the simple life he had as a child. 'When I was young, you went out and made up your own little games, or you grabbed a football or drew a hopscotch frame on the ground and got on with it. Children were freer then.'

Born on 8 November 1932, 'right opposite from what is now the Dundrum shopping centre', he recalls how it was almost countryside back then. 'There was nothing but fields between Windy Arbour and Dundrum. There was even a herd of magnificent Jersey cows in Airfield, looked after by my Uncle Joe.

'My earliest memories are of the Sisters of Charity school in Milltown. I would have been there until I was seven. It was a lovely school. I remember looking at a paper just a few years back, and there was a funeral, it was a Ms Wright, she was my teacher. She was a pleasant person, but she seemed to me to be very old at the time. And yet here I am, only six or seven years ago, and I see her death in the paper. I couldn't believe it. I suddenly realised that the woman who had taught me over eighty years ago and who seemed to be so old must have been only a young woman at the time.

There was nothing but fields between Windy Arbour and Dundrum. There was even a herd of magnificent Jersey cows in Airfield, looked after by my Uncle Joe.

'I remember when I was about six years old, walking with my mother in the nearby village of Milltown. There were cottages there. It was a beautiful day, so the doors of the cottages were open, and we heard the radio announcing, "We are at war with Germany." It always stuck in my mind. My mum couldn't believe it. She knew there were difficulties, she was a member of the women's union at the time. My father and mother were both in trade union movements. I remember her talking about it all to my father when we got home.

'The war didn't affect me as a child, except in small ways. We had the rationing but I had two cousins who were radio officers in the merchant navy. They travelled back and forth across the world. We had tea rationing and my cousin Joey Treacy came back home from New York with a big plywood box of orange pekoe tea. We drank our way through it with the neighbours and it lasted for ages.

'My Aunt Nan lived in Carrickfergus. My two brothers and I exchanged holidays with my cousins there. I remember seeing Belgian soldiers coming back from the war in an awful state. This would have been around 1943. My aunt had three of them rehabilitating with her. I remember coming in after playing tennis with my cousins one day and my aunt was in a bit of a state. She said that Joey, my Aunt Polly's son, was missing in action. He was on a convey to Malta, and his boat was torpedoed in the middle of the Mediterranean. He was never found. He would have only been in his twenties.

'As children, we played football on the roads. There were very few cars on the road back then, just the odd bus every half hour or so. We would have played hopscotch and hide and seek.

'My brothers and I always had a new suit for Christmas. We were very well dressed because our father was a tailor. In the 1940s, through a combination of lack of money and rationing, clothes had to be recycled or handed down. Our family was very lucky, Dad could get remnants of cloth in the factory where he worked. Even when I emigrated in the early fifties I had on a new suit, and two in my case. He used to reverse overcoats using what was the inside of the coat; as it was protected by the lining, it would end up looking as if it were a new coat, giving many more years' wear. Even guards came to him when they got a new issue of overcoats, they would keep the old one and my father would remodel the new issue to give a better shape and fit.

I remember coming in after playing tennis with my cousins one day and my aunt was in a bit of a state. She said that Joey, my Aunt Polly's son, was missing in action. He was never found. He would have only been in his twenties.

'At Christmas, neighbours would come over and join in the festivities. And we would visit our aunt who lived nearby. We would have hooleys. There would be music and that. It was a divil of a house for arguments though, usually about politics! We must remember there was no TV, computers, or mobiles, only dance halls or the radio. So most of the fun had to be created by yourself and your friends.

'I had a great group of friends in the forties and fifties, both fellows and girls. We did everything together, played sport – girls camogie and the fellows soccer for Sandyford. We were all members of the church choir, and the dramatic society in Sandyford – many's the time playing to full houses in Sandyford library, which would be a theatre for the night. Dancing on a Sunday night in Butler's of The Scalp, Kilternan or the Legion Hall in Enniskerry. Birthdays we celebrated at home with Georgie Kavanagh, one of the lads on the piano. Starting on a Saturday night and ending when we had to go play a match on the Sunday morning.

'We had a beautiful gramophone I got in 1947, and I will always remember it because I got it the night the terrible snow started in the early part of March that year. We didn't get out of that snow until nearly May. I remember going to a funeral in Sandyford, and we actually took the coffin on a sleigh! They were going to Kilgobbin for the burial, and don't ask me how they dug the grave.

'But as young people, we had a great winter that year. There is a big field opposite Stepaside garda station, and there was a big hill. We built a toboggan out of a large piece of galvanised tin. It took about six of us! There was a bush at the bottom of the hill, and as we neared it whoever was at the front would say "Off!" and we would all tumble off because there was no way to stop it.

'There was not a great emphasis on religion in our home although we went to mass. However, our group of friends got together for carol singing every year, and on a Holy Thursday we said prayers in seven churches starting at Milltown, the Sisters of Charity convent, Milltown, Beechwood Avenue, Donnybrook, Stillorgan, Dundrum and finishing at Sandyford. We also went to the Rosary on a Monday night. I would question if it were for the religion or the craic, the friends getting together for a day or the evening out; perhaps both!'

Contemplating how life has changed since his early years, Tom talks of the simplicity of childhood, and how children today are 'locked into technology. They don't understand what you can make and enjoy yourself, the simple things. They are too old now, as children.

'Religion is very different now too. In my day it was strict. You were a Catholic and you went to mass and there was no opting out. There is a lot you can say that is wrong with religion, but the one thing about the church that can get lost in the bureaucracy and all that is the calmness and peace that you can get from being in it.

'I would like to see my grandchildren's generation keeping our religious traditions. Life has gotten too fast.'

We had a beautiful gramophone I got in 1947, and I will always remember it because I got it the night the terrible snow started in the early part of March that year. We didn't get out of that snow until nearly May. I remember going to a funeral in Sandyford, and we actually took the coffin on a sleigh!

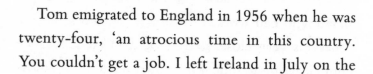

Tom emigrated to England in 1956 when he was twenty-four, 'an atrocious time in this country. You couldn't get a job. I left Ireland in July on the

St Columba from Dún Laoghaire – it was a beautiful summer's evening – surrounded by many like me. It was the thing at the time, to emigrate. I was very lucky, I had seen this job advertised for British Rail. They had an office in North Wall, and that was where the interview was held. So I actually got the job before I went. Then, England was still recovering from the war. The number of men they had lost was quite considerable. British Rail had a college in Watford, and I was sent there to get my diploma as a work study engineer.'

Tom met his first wife, Margaret Ryan, in 1956. Margaret was a beautiful dancer, and the couple spent many happy times on the ballroom scene before they married in 1957. They had three children and the family returned to Ireland in 1970, when Tom joined the Irish Congress of Trade Unions work study section.

Tom and Margaret, who is now sadly passed, have twelve grandchildren and Tom recalls the special joy when their first, Matthew, was born, and the sense of a new miracle each time another one came along. In 1999, Tom remarried, and Miriam, a palliative nurse who had worked with Margaret through her illness, is very close to the grandchildren. If Tom could leave his grandchildren any advice, it would be to live their own lives. 'In recent years there has been such a domination from parents, putting pressure on their kids to push them down a particular road. We should try and get it through to children that school years are just a time for learning and expanding their minds. At the end of the day, the Leaving Cert is just an exam. There are a lot of youngsters who are forced down a particular road, and we need to get it through to them that it is not necessary. I would say to my grandchildren, "There is a life outside of your schooldays."'

Over the years Tom would write postcards to his grandchildren from the various places he visited, and when asked how he would like to be remembered, it is holidays spent with them that come to mind: 'They're great kids. I would like to think that they would remember the little gestures and our friendship and all the fun times we had together on holidays in different places. I hope they know that I am here for them.'

Grandchildren from age thirty-one to seven:
Matthew, Liam, Conor, Ryan, Ian, Megan,
Nolan, Cian, Maria, Lucia & David

A Quaker Story

YVONNE TRAYNOR

Interfaith minister Yvonne Traynor became a grandmother early. At age fifty-seven, in 2014, Elsie arrived in the world, 'my only granddaughter and I would live and die for her, we have an incredibly strong bond, thank God'.

Now a grandmother of five, Yvonne's earliest memories feature the arrival home of her newborn sister Hilary, when Yvonne was three and a half. 'She was dressed in lemon yellow and my mother had a maroon suitcase. When we were very young we had a fairly good childhood. I had no brothers so the boys on the estate treated me like a sister. We played all the usual games like red rover; queenie-eye-oh, who has the ball?; skipping; hopscotch; tennis in the back garden; teddy bear picnics and water fights!

Today, in our sixties, I am still friendly with most of those boys, we even go on holidays together.'

Yvonne's interest in interfaith relations began early. 'I am Church of Ireland, I was baptised, confirmed and married as Church of Ireland. However, my mum left my name on the Quaker register until I was twenty-one, in case I opted to go to a meeting for regular worship.' So the young Yvonne belonged to two youth clubs, the Quaker youth club in Rathfarnham and the Zion youth club in Rathgar. 'My one ambition was to let Roman Catholics come to the youth club, which was quite a huge deal then, and I succeeded with both of them!'

Her parents had been married in the Quaker meeting house in Churchtown. 'The funny thing about it is that after my father died, my mother got baptised and I stood for her in the confirmation, she was one of the last adults to get confirmed in St Anne's in Dawson Street. I think possibly the reason for that was because she wanted to go into a particular nursing home in Ranelagh!'

Now sixty-five, Yvonne has no qualms about disclosing her age. 'My husband Leo died when he was only forty-two, so I think I am very lucky to be still alive.' The couple met in Murphy's in

Rathgar, and he proposed to her four months on. 'I was nineteen and he was twenty-three. We were lucky, we were just under twenty years married. We have three lovely children.' But it was hard after her husband's death at such a young age, and Yvonne is no stranger to the everyday struggle faced by so many today, the challenge of making ends meet.

We played all the usual games
like red rover; queenie-eye-oh, who
has the ball?; skipping; hopscotch;
tennis in the back garden; teddy
bear picnics and water fights!

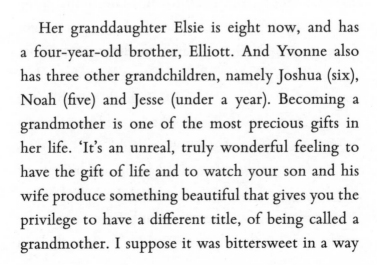

Her granddaughter Elsie is eight now, and has a four-year-old brother, Elliott. And Yvonne also has three other grandchildren, namely Joshua (six), Noah (five) and Jesse (under a year). Becoming a grandmother is one of the most precious gifts in her life. 'It's an unreal, truly wonderful feeling to have the gift of life and to watch your son and his wife produce something beautiful that gives you the privilege to have a different title, of being called a grandmother. I suppose it was bittersweet in a way because Leo would have loved it, he would have been in his element, he was a larger-than-life person and he would have just been so proud.'

Yvonne studied with the OneSpirit Interfaith Foundation in the UK to become an interfaith minister. 'All my grandchildren at that time came to my graduation. They are actually very proud of me.'

Interfaith ministers are not allowed in traditional churches, 'so basically it means that I am the temple of the people and I represent the people so I can be anywhere. I have done ceremonies on the Hill of Tara or I would do blessings, I would do a lot of things with the undertakers. Say, for example, a family don't really want a Catholic funeral, I would very often do the blessing of the closing of the coffin just to give it a little bit of balance, and if I do a funeral ceremony I go straight to the crematorium. I also conduct naming ceremonies for babies.'

After my father died, my mother
got baptised and I stood for her in
the confirmation, she was one of the
last adults to get confirmed in
St Anne's in Dawson Street.

Her son and daughter-in-law emigrated to Canada three years ago, and Yvonne regularly visits. 'I think it is very important to be with the grandchildren when they are young because once they get to be teenagers, really other teenagers are the only things in their lives that they're mad about!'

Yvonne says she would love to pass on to her grand-children a love of the outdoors, and an appreciation of what is truly valuable in life. 'Not really monetary values and just to really respect people; life is all about doing things and just giving people time and spending time with people and being with people and loving people.'

And as for nuggets of wisdom? 'I would like them to know that you don't have to have a whole heap of money to be happy. The simple things are best. The boys here love making banana bread with me, we do crafting, we learn about other countries, we were doing Scotland last week, they thought it was hilarious that men wear kilts!'

And how would Yvonne like her grandchildren to remember her? 'As a nana who would try anything, which they know I would. I mean, I did a shark cage dive less than ten years ago with my son when he was in Australia. I taught myself how to paddleboard last summer. I would like them to have felt that they could talk to me about anything and that I was always a very safe person to talk to and that I always gave them the time that I felt was necessary and I put them first. I would really like them to remember me like that and that I love them very, very much. The best jewels around my neck are the arms of my grandchildren.'

Grandchildren from age eight to eleven months:
Elsie, Joshua, Noah, Elliott & Jesse

The Stones, The Who ...
and the Legion of Mary

DEAGLÁN DE BRÉADÚN

Journalist Deaglán de Bréadún started life in Enniscorthy, Wexford, in a house with no television. 'My mother was worried it would distract us from our studies. We didn't get the television until the World Cup of 1966, when my older brothers insisted on getting it.'

The family later moved to Dublin. 'I was the son of a guard in Wexford, so I think there were always some reservations [locally] with regard to people like me. In Dublin, though, no one knew who we were. It was more relaxed in that sense, but you were more aware of class differences. In the country, the gap between rich and poor wasn't as obvious as it was in the city. We lived in Ranelagh, but it was near enough to Mount Pleasant, which at the time was a rough enough area. I remember one of the local lads from Mount Pleasant declaring war on me as a child!'

My mother was worried it would distract us from our studies. We didn't get the television until the World Cup of 1966, when my brothers insisted on getting it.

Deaglán recalls his love of reading, enshrined from early on. 'I read night and day. I used to get books out of the children's library in Rathmines, read them overnight and bring them back the next day. I don't think there's as much of that going on these days. Everything is online, which is both a blessing and a curse.'

Deaglán remembers the arrival of his American aunt and cousins in Enniscorthy when he was about five. 'The visitors had taken a boat from New York to Cobh. 'This American car that they'd brought with them pulled up outside. I'll never forget it. It was like a movie. My father never learned to drive, and my mother only learned in her sixties, so we couldn't believe it. All the kids on the street were amazed.'

He came from a religious household, where the Rosary was said every night and Deaglán had his own designated decade: 'The Finding of the Child Jesus in the Temple – that was my one, that I would lead.'

Schooldays in CBS Synge Street were happy, though 'there was a bit of slagging, with humorous intent, picking on others, but I gave as good as I got. There was corporal punishment back then, a lot of it. The leather straps were in fairly regular use.'

But growing up as a teenager in Dublin was very exciting. 'I saw The Rolling Stones on stage when Brian Jones was still alive. I saw The Who when Keith Moon was still alive. I missed The Beatles, because I was in the Legion of Mary and was busy doing some voluntary work for them that evening! A friend of mine said the screaming was unbearable at that gig so it wasn't too much fun. I think he was just trying to cheer me up. There were all the protests about the Vietnam war at the time. Woodstock was on in upstate New York, and there was such a buzz in the world, a hippie era, it was that kind of time. There was so much going on in Dublin, beat clubs and tennis hops and everything, there was a great music scene, great bands, and there was a pop culture that was very life-enhancing.'

> In the country, the gap between rich and poor wasn't as obvious as it was in the city. We lived in Ranelagh, but it was near enough to Mount Pleasant, which at the time was a rough enough area. I remember one of the local lads from Mount Pleasant declaring war on me as a child!

After school, Deaglán went to UCD to study arts in 1967. 'I got caught up in the "gentle revolution", a wave of student protest. There were big protests in France and the US about the Vietnam war, and it caught on in UCD and Trinity. We got enraptured by the idea that we could change the world and make it more just and equal. This was quite a distraction from our student work!'

Deaglán met his future wife, Maria, when they were teenagers working summer jobs at Chivers jam factory. 'We were on the strawberry section. Strawberries would come in, and Maria would pick out the bad strawberries and throw them away. I was at the other end of the production line, and

I would pack the tins into crates, and they would head off to the shops. One evening it was very noisy, and you couldn't hear what was being said, so I looked at Maria, held a can up to my head, pointed at my eye, then her, then the door, so I was saying, "Can I see you home?" Anyway, we went on a date and the rest is history.'

In a journalism career that has taken him far and wide, from *Irish Times* foreign-language correspondent to northern editor, Deaglán considers the changing nature of the newspaper business over the years. 'I think print newspapers are going to become like magazines now. The weekend editions will be still published, but the weekday ones are going to become a thing of the past. People are getting their news online now. I think it is a pity, I think the standard of print journalism would be higher than online.'

Deaglán and Maria are the proud grandparents of five – Beatrice, Juliet, Cal, Louis and Matthew (and another one on the way) – and parents of four children, Erica, Cillian, Ronan and Olwen. 'Erica had our first grandchild, Beatrice. She was born in the Coombe, and every-thing went according to plan. It was just brilliant, we were so happy that she was born, and healthy and everything. We were so excited to have a grandchild in the family. I hope my grandchildren have as happy a life as I had. I am happily married, with a lovely family, and a job I love and am happy in. I want that for them too.

There was so much going on in
Dublin, beat clubs and tennis hops
and everything, there was a great music
scene, great bands, and there was a pop
culture that was very life-enhancing.

'I think bonds between family, between children and grandchildren, are hugely important. Those bonds are beneficial for the morale and mental health of the grandparents, and for the grandchildren as well. I never met my grandparents. I would hope that my grandchildren would remember me as funny and entertaining and a good laugh.'

Grandchildren from age seven to three:
Beatrice, Cal, Matthew, Juliette & Louis

Dressing Up for Church

PATRICIA NARKIE
NARTEY DWYER

Irish grandmother Patricia Narkie Nartey Dwyer was born in Accra in Ghana but has lived in Ireland since she was eighteen years old. Her dad, Edward, a timber merchant, travelled a lot, so the family moved within Ghana. Her earliest memories come from Nkawkaw 'when I was about eight months old, and I was sitting in a wheelbarrow, and there was a man who was cutting down loads of bananas around the house'.

Patricia and her seven siblings (four boys and three girls) spent most of their childhood in Takoradi in the estern Region. 'We lived in a huge house – well, it seemed huge to me at that time! We had a lot of land, and I would come home and play, and my dad would come home from work and play football with us in the garden. My mother, Emilia, used to play hopscotch with us, drawing the figures on the cement and we would jump with her.

'We didn't wander off too much as kids. Opposite the house there was a sports club, and we would go and play tennis, and the Atlantic Ocean was near us too. Every Saturday afternoon, my father would go fishing and bring us along and we would swim.'

As well as playtime, however, there was also work. 'Every child had their little chores they had to do at the weekend, especially on Saturday. One would scrub the toilet, another would make the beds, that sort of thing. But you had time to play; we would play with our dolls, plaiting their hair, and the boys would be playing conkers. Friends would come and visit too.

'My father was a philanthropist, so he would have loads of cousins and friends come and stay with us when they were attending college. My mother was an African textile trader, she traded in beautiful African prints. She would have the materials delivered to the house, and people would come to buy them. She was working from home long before everyone else was! And she was minding her children too and making dinners and everything.'

Religion played an important part in Patricia's upbringing. 'We would dress up on Sunday and go to church and we said our prayers every night with my parents before bed. We were Presbyterian. My secondary school was multidenominational, with lots of religions, but the boys went to a St Augustin Brothers school. We girls went to a mixed school because my father wanted us to know what men were like, so we wouldn't take any nonsense off them when we grew up!'

One of Patricia's relatives proved to be her inspiration, career-wise. 'Growing up in Ireland is different to Ghana. I came to Ireland at 18 to do my nursing. I had an aunt who was an EMT nurse, and she travelled the world and then came home, and I was fascinated by her. She brought me into a hospital one Saturday afternoon to see an appendectomy, and I was hooked! I thought it was fascinating watching the nurses working, I decided then that that was what I wanted to do!'

In Ghana, Patricia remembers how the family structure was hugely important. 'Your family was like a community. You could go to sleep in an empty house, and when you woke up the next morning there could be somebody at the end of the bed! We had our grandparents in and out of our house all the time. We would have one set of grandparents come and stay for a year and then leave, and then another set come in after that. When my parents were travelling, we could be shipped off for a few weeks to the grandparents too. We always had them in our lives until they passed away.'

We girls went to a mixed school because my father wanted us to know what men were like, so we wouldn't take any nonsense off them when we grew up!'

Partying and a sense of fun was a feature of her family life, Patricia recalls. 'Ours was a house with lots of parties. My father was a businessman, so he always had to invite people over. After Easter Monday, we would have a little get-together, my mother would cook, and we would have neighbours over. We would also celebrate the festival week in August, and at Christmas, and all the birthdays as well … we never stopped having parties really!

'In Africa, it wouldn't be like a formal fancy dinner party, with everyone dressed up and everything, it would be quite casual. As kids, we would go to bed early during the party, unless it was New Year's, where we were allowed to stay up until midnight. The rest of the time, our granny Theodora would shove us back into bed if she caught us poking our heads out!'

Coming to Ireland was a learning experience for Patricia, in a number of ways. 'My mother made our clothes, and she also had a seamstress who made clothes for special occasions. We were very lucky girls, we never wanted for anything. When I came to Ireland it was a shock, going from having everything handed to you to having to do everything for yourself! My aunt had prepared me for that though, she had told me I would have to fend for myself. The language was also a shock, I spoke English but I was not prepared for the accents! There were so many accents, from Donegal to Kerry to Mayo; I couldn't understand them, and I used to say, "Can you slow down, please!?"

> The language was also a shock, I spoke English but I was not prepared for the accents! There were so many accents, from Donegal to Kerry to Mayo.

'When I came to Ireland, there was no racism that I saw and I never experienced any racism raising my children. People were so nice. People of colour in Ireland back then were either a priest, a doctor or a nurse. My father had a friend in Ballyferriter in County Kerry and we visited him in 1978, walked into the pub, and the whole pub stopped and turned around. They had never seen a black person before. I was only in Ireland about a week then. They weren't being rude at all, and they got my dad drunk, they were so generous!'

Patricia's chosen career was to lead to a very important encounter. 'I was training in the Richmond hospital when I came here, and I stayed in the nurses' home. I met my husband at one of these nurses' dances, you know. His name is Dermot Dwyer. We got married in Ireland in 1984, and we had three girls, Sarah, Alison and Ciara. My husband was a mechanic, but he is too old for that now, so he drives a taxi!'

Being present at the birth of her first grandchild was very special for Patricia. 'Our daughter Sarah lived in Australia for a while so our first grandchild, Lucas, was born there. I was in the room when he was born so it was just wonderful to see the next generation. I am a midwife myself. It was very emotional; I used to cry when I would deliver babies that aren't even related to me so to see my daughter having a child … it was just wonderful.

'We have five grandchildren now and another one on the way. I don't know if it is a boy or a girl, the parents don't want to know and I am delighted, I love a surprise!'

Today Patricia and her husband live with their daughter Sarah in a 'granny' flat attached to Sarah's house. 'I mind the kids when Sarah is going somewhere, but I say, "I am retired now so it is only two days a week!" When I had my children, my mother came all the way from Africa to help me for six months and stayed with me until I was on my feet and then went back. I felt that if someone did that for me, I should do that for someone else.

> In Africa there were always people
> around looking after you, your own family.
> But here in Ireland, I was working, and I
> had to find other people to mind my
> children, which is different to Ghana.

'In Africa there were always people around looking after you, your own family. But here in Ireland, I was working, and I had to find other people to mind my children, which is different to Ghana.

You have to take other people's values in, and respect other people's values. Childminding here is different. In Africa, you wouldn't call it that because it was your extended family, your cousins and that. I never had a childminder because my mother was at home all the time, and if she was going somewhere, my granny or my aunt or my cousin would come.'

Does Patricia have any particular philosophy she would like to pass on to her grandchildren? 'I believe that in this life, you have to have faith in something. You have to be good to people, and people will be good to you. Do unto others as others will do unto you! Siblings fight all the time, so I say to my grandchildren, "If you don't want someone to do that to you, don't do it to them, it will come back and bite you in the bum!" They will be writing that on my headstone!

'Happiness is the most important thing. Money doesn't matter, as long as you are doing what you love. You never know where life is going to take you. Look at me, ending up in Ireland coming from Africa. My grandkids might end up all over the world.'

Grandchildren from age eight to nine months:
Lucas, Emelia, twins Elijah & Myles, & Isaiah

Friday Was
Sardines and Crisps

JOHN FITZPATRICK &
CATHY FITZPATRICK

'My grandmother, Lily Lucas, worked as an usherette in the Gaiety theatre for fifty years. When my mother would go shopping, she would leave me in with Lily to watch the pantomimes. I saw them all about six or seven times!'

This is one of the earliest memories of seventy-three-year-old Dublin taxi driver John FitzPatrick, who grew up in Milltown as one of the nine children of Jack and Millie FitzPatrick: 'Jean, John, Catherine, Anne, Brenda, Avril, Theresa, Brian and Sheila. It was great growing up in a big family. Our grandmother, Lily (or Lil), also lived with us but we didn't know that when we were growing up, we thought she was our aunt!'

Lily had given birth to Millie in England in the 1920s at a time when an unplanned pregnancy was regarded as a disaster. Millie's father was in the RAF and already married, but the couple (who had no children of their own) asked to adopt the baby girl. Lily agreed and left the baby and returned to Ireland. But six weeks later, with the support of her parents, she went back and took the baby home with her. When Millie was married with her own children, Lily went to live with them as their much-loved 'aunt'. It was only when the grandchildren were in their twenties that they discovered Lily, who they'd lived with all their lives, was actually their grandmother.

My grandmother, Lily Lucas, worked
as an usherette in the Gaiety theatre for
fifty years. When my mother would go
shopping, she would leave me in with
Lily to watch the pantomimes. I saw
them all about six or seven times!

'I wasn't annoyed with my parents when I found out,' John says, 'it didn't bother me at all really.' His sister, seventy-year-old Cathy, remembers Lily as 'a lovely, lovely woman. She was the kindest person I ever met.'

Both siblings have strong memories of what life was like when they were young, a casual world where children had the time of their lives, playing and exploring from dawn to dusk. 'We didn't have a television but we had loads of friends and we would go out all day, swimming in the Dodder, or picking blackberries in late summer,' says John.

'The river ran behind our house,' says Cathy, 'there were fields there too, it was a bit of a swamp. We used to call it Azouka Island, because we were kids and wanted to be exotic! We would make bows and arrows, I think we used willow branches, they are very flexible. We would be firing them at each other, pretending to be cowboys and Indians. We had very creative minds back then. We would play shop with wood and stones for money. I don't really remember having toys, maybe a doll or a teddy. John made a trolley once. He got the wheels off an old pram, and got some scrap wood and made a little trolley. We used to push each other around on it.

'We would head out in the morning and be gone all day and we wouldn't come back until dinner time. We would walk for miles and miles and be off playing and picking blackberries. We would bring an empty tin, like a tin of USA biscuits, and we would put the blackberries in that, and bring it home and make jam. Then we used to pick fruit for Fruitfields [the jam company]. I wasn't allowed to pick the strawberries, they didn't trust me! We were paid a pittance, a couple of pennies really. It was child labour!' Around the same time, twelve-year-old John started working as a caddy in Milltown golf course making five shillings a round.

We all had roller-skates, about fifteen or twenty kids on the road, we would hold each other by the hips and go along like a big caterpillar. I was leading one time and one kid fell and dragged everyone else down!

Sweets were very restricted. 'We would only get them at the weekend,' says Cathy. 'My granny would buy us a packet of crisps on a Friday, so Friday would be sardines in tomato sauce and then my crisps! My dad used to bring in a Trigger bar or some sort of chocolate on a Friday. At Christmas you would get an apple and an orange, and a few chocolates from the Cadbury's chocolate box, and then your toy or your doll.'

'We didn't have holidays as children,' says John, 'but sometimes we would get the lend of a car and drive out to Howth or something. Maybe the younger sisters and Brian might have, but us older kids didn't get proper holidays!'

Cathy remembers the roller-skating craze when she was about twelve. 'We all had roller-skates, about fifteen or twenty kids on the road, we would hold each other by the hips and go along like a big caterpillar. I was leading one time and one kid fell and dragged everyone else down! That was a bit of a disaster, but we loved roller-skating.

'We would play handball against the wall as well, playing with two balls and then three balls and progressing it that way. It was very fun. We played "beds" as well, with an empty polish tin. We would draw out numbers from one to twelve. You'd get used to your polish tin and the movements, and we wouldn't want to lose that particular one!

'There were great characters when we were growing up, like the rag-and-bone man. He had a donkey and cart. He would have jars and boxes of broken rock, sticks of rock. He would come along, and we would rush in to our mothers and say, "Have you got any old clothes or bottles or jars for us to give to him?" We would give him a piece of clothing or a jar, and he would give us a piece of rock in return. We used to love that. I sometimes tell my grandchildren these stories and they look at me in amazement, because it is so different to their lives now.

'There were other men with horses and carts then, the milkman or the bread man. Sometimes the horse would poo on the road, and people would run out with a bucket to try and collect it, because they put it on their rose bushes! That wouldn't happen today. A kid wouldn't go near it!'

On the subject of religion, John says his parents were very devout. 'Millie went to mass every day, and I was an altar boy for a while, a couple of years. I don't think it was a good idea to instil fear into children, thinking they were going to hell and all that. I didn't encourage my own children to go to mass.' And Cathy recalls Aunt Lil 'who was always blessing us with holy water. I am not exaggerating when I say we would be in our beds and we would get a splash! It could be in the morning, when we came in from school, before bed … There was a holy water font just inside the door.'

> We all had roller-skates, about fifteen
> or twenty kids on the road, we would
> hold each other by the hips and go
> along like a big caterpillar. I was
> leading one time and one kid fell
> and dragged everyone else down!

Cathy remembers huge family Christmases. 'Sometimes I look back at photographs of the Christmas trees we had, and I crack up laughing, they were so small compared to now! We used to make all our own decorations out of crinkly paper. And we would string them up on the ceiling as well … and have a candle in the window – talk about a fire hazard!'

But there were logistics involved in feeding such a big family. 'We were always very well fed. My dad would do the Sunday dinner, cook turkey and ham and mushy peas and roast potatoes and all that. We would be in one room, says Cathy, and my parents would be in the kitchen, and your name would be called. You'd go into the kitchen, and my dad would be there with a plate – "Do you want peas? Do you want potatoes?" Like a canteen!'

> We would walk for miles and miles
> and be off playing and picking
> blackberries. We would bring an
> empty tin, like a tin of USA biscuits,
> and we would put the blackberries in
> that, and bring it home and make jam.

Schooldays for John were tough. 'I started in Synge Street at nine years of age, and got beaten around the place every day with the leather strap. Major corporal punishment went on every day. I would go home and my father would ask, "How many biffs did you get today?" He never made a complaint, though, I think he would have thought we deserved it.'

Cathy attended Dundrum Vocational School (now Dundrum College of Further Education), and one day, aged fifteen, she was called out of class by the head teacher, 'and she sends me for an interview for a job as a copy typist in an office in a garage in Dundrum and that's what I did! But it's like no one asked me, neither my parents or teacher or headmistress – no one said, "Would you like to stay in school? Would you like any further education?" It was just, "Get them a job, get them out working." So Cathy worked in a series of office jobs in Dublin and London, including eleven years in St Columba's College in Dublin. Then she discovered healing therapies and trained in polarity therapy and massage. In the meantime, she got married to Norman Butler and they had two children, although they are now divorced.

The family had a great-uncle, Christy 'Tippy' Hackett, who owned the Jewish bakery, the Bretzel, on Lennox Street in Portobello, and as a schoolboy John was a regular visitor. 'You'd get slices of gur cake as big as your hand for two pennies! I used to go to the bakery every day during the week. I would get off class at noon, and I'd get the twelve bus up Killeen Road every day for lunch and my grandfather would have me chopping sticks!

'Then when the dog had puppies, he'd make me cut the puppies' tails as well. You'd tie a little bandage around the tail, as close as you could, and then you'd get a halfpenny, and you'd cut the tail to the length of the halfpenny. It was important to get the tail cut to the right length. That's all changed now.

'I went to my grandparents' place for lunch instead of my own house because it was much closer to Synge Street. Where we lived in Milltown was pretty much countryside at that time. I have the last ever ticket from the train station out there in 1958.

'During the summertime when I was on school holidays, my grandfather and I would plant onions and lettuce and cut sticks to the right size and all that. There were hardly any boy grandchildren, out of nineteen grandchildren, he only had five boys and one of them lived in Wales, so maybe that's why I did so much for them!

'As a teenager, I joined the reserve navy. The FCA was the army, and we were the navy part of it. On Mondays, we would go down to Cathal Brugha barracks, and learn how to march and all that. We would march in the Easter parade every year. On a Friday we would go down with our rifles, real rifles with bullets in the magazine! We would go down to the ESB to patrol, I think it might have been because of threats from the IRA. Sort of a nighttime guard, and it would be in the freezing cold as well.'

John served his time as a sheet metalworker, 'and then I went over to London and married my first wife, Annie [since deceased] when I was twenty-three. We had four children, all girls: Tara, Louise, Emma and Gail. I was married to Annie for eight years, and I've been thirty-five years with my present wife, Margaret. We have one girl together called Ciara. I have six grandchildren; James is my eldest grandson, he is about twenty-three. My youngest grandchild is Ruby, she is sixteen months.

'Life isn't getting any better for children these days, trying to keep a roof over their head and all,' says John, who is all for thrift at the end of life. 'I don't want to spend money on a grave, I think it's a waste. I'm going to get cremated, and they can do what they like with my ashes — they can put them around the roses if they want to.'

Cathy has very specific wishes for her grand-children and their futures. 'I would like them to grow up in safety, in peace. I would like them to remember me, to know that they were truly well loved, that I couldn't love them any more than I do and that I did everything I could for them. I talk a lot to Juliette and Dylan and I tell them, "Don't always believe what your teacher tells you or what you read in the paper." I say to them, "Read and learn how to do your own research." And I tell them always to respect themselves and other people. I tell them God is love, and always to be honest and to do the right thing. I did my best for myself, for them and for my family.'

John's grandchildren from age twenty-one to eight months: Daryl, James, John, Amy, Matheus, Gabriella, Jack, Annie, Ruby & Bonnie.

Cathy's grandchildren from age twenty-one to six: Dylan, Juliette, Bradley, Leila & Jack

Playing the Bagpipes
at the Olympics

ARMELLE GOULET

Armelle Marie Levenez came to Ireland from Rennes in north-western France when she was four and a half years old. 'My earliest memory of living there was of my great-grandmother. She was in a wheelchair, and she wasn't able to eat nuts, it would upset her stomach. But there were walnut trees in the garden, and she would get me to go and get walnuts for her, and I would get in trouble! She was my father's granny, and I loved her.

'We lived in a house called La Bondoniere. Those were the good days. My father, Yann [Goulet], was working as a sculptor then, he had worked on the Exhibition in Paris. He also played the bagpipes at the Olympic Games in 1936 in Berlin. The Bretons were asked to take part in the opening, as well as the Irish. There was a group from Galway too. Daddy was there with the Bretons in 1936, representing France. He was still a student at that time. He and my mother weren't married yet, she worked for a newspaper.

'All of those years were a bit blurred, they weren't talked about a lot. There was a lot going on in the family though, my father's political goings-on, Breton liberation. My mother's mother was a tough woman. She held it against my mother that she married my father, she never wanted to speak to us, because of my father's politics.

> My father was working as a sculptor then, he had worked on the Exhibition in Paris. He also played the bagpipes at the Olympic Games in 1936 in Berlin. The Bretons were asked to take part in the opening, as well as the Irish.

'We came to Ireland because of my father's political views. During those Olympic Games they met Goebbels. They shook hands and photographs were taken, and my father was then accused of being a Nazi collaborator, and the French government said that they had proof of it because of this photo.

There was a whole thing in Brittany, some Bretons went on the German side and others didn't, and my father didn't. He was tried in absentia as a collaborator and he was sentenced to death. That is why we came to Ireland. It was May 1947, after the war. My father had to get out, and he didn't want to get out without us. Myself, the eldest, and my baby brother Herve. Between myself and Herve we had a sister who died at birth. Annique was her name. They reckoned that it was the stress of it all on my mother that caused the tragedy. My father was in jail at the time. Herve was nine months old when we came to Ireland.'

Armelle's father was a great admirer of Pádraig Pearse and this is the reason the family came to Ireland. 'He had Dan Breen's book *My Fight for Irish Freedom*, which I think had been translated into French. He had some English but he didn't speak it well.

'If you were accused of something, you lost all rights to inheritance, but a few others went back to France and got a pardon. My father was very stubborn, and said, "I am not going to go back to France and look for a pardon and apologise for something that I didn't do, I never collaborated."'

The family arrived via Belfast, and were met by a man from Dalkey, Oscar McCarthy Willis, in whose home they stayed until they rented their own home in Bray on the seafront and later on Herbert Road in Dublin 4. 'At that stage, my father had done the Custom House memorial sculpture, and he was beginning to become known, both as a sculptor and an art teacher. He had rented this plot in Bray, and built his studio there. The first part was for the pupils, and then behind long curtains was his area. It was a big, messy studio, with a big armchair by the stove.

'My childhood was very much "home, school, home". My younger sister, Brigid, was born in Ireland. She goes by Bidou. We didn't speak English, so I didn't understand anything that was going on in school. I remember coming home and saying, "I need to pick a name for my confirmation" and my father saying, "No you don't, you've just misunderstood again!" So the day came when they were asking for the names in class, and I wanted Anne, but I said to myself, *What's the English for Anne? Elizabeth?,* so I picked Elizabeth!

'I did make some friends, but I never really played with them apart from one girl, Patricia. We did roller-skating along the seafront and we went swimming too, I was a member of the swimming club in Bray. My father was a brilliant long-distance swimmer.

During those Olympic Games they met Goebbels. They shook hands and photographs were taken, and my father was then accused of being a Nazi collaborator, and the French government said that they had proof of it because of this photo.

~⌒⌒~

'I loved my father, but he was very, very strict. I was the eldest, and it was tough. I remember Aer Lingus were looking for air hostesses, and I wasn't allowed apply. My father said, "I didn't send you to the Holy Child [secondary school, Killiney] to be serving coffee!" No way would he approve of it.'

In time though Armelle got a job in Aer Lingus as a ground hostess. 'Four of us were picked to be *Cailín Fáiltes*, and we used to have fresh carnations for our buttonholes every morning. It was a fabulous job. We had a beautiful uniform that we helped design.'

It was there she met her husband Don, who worked in ground operations. 'It wasn't love at first sight for me anyway. He pursued me, he was very kind, and then we fell in love, much to the horror of my father, as Don was twenty years older than me!

'I didn't know if my father was going to come to the wedding or not. In the photographs, you can tell from his face he wasn't happy! It was a small wedding.'

On 11 November 1967, Armistice Day, the couple's first child, Armellig, was born, but sadly the baby was not well. 'She was baptised straight away and then driven to Crumlin where she was operated on immediately. I never got to hold her. I remember seeing a nurse holding her and feeding her, but I wasn't allowed. I thought it was the cruellest thing possible. She was in an incubator with gadgets on her. It was awful.' Tragically, Armellig died less than a month later, on 2 December. 'All that time, I never got to hold her.' She is buried with Don's family in an old Franciscan friary. Armelle and Don went on to have two sons, Erig and Ronan.

Armelle says the best day of her life was when her granddaughter, Thea, was born. 'I was excited when my daughter-in-law, Debbie, was pregnant, but I wasn't half as excited as when I found out she was going to be having a little girl! I went to my Zumba class, and when I got out of the class there was a voice message from Ronan saying they were on their way to Holles Street! I headed straight in and Ronan came out to say it was a girl. Oh my God. I melted when I saw her. I was just ecstatic. I have photos of the first time I held her. She was just beautiful.

I remember Aer Lingus were looking
for air hostesses, and I wasn't allowed
apply. My father said, "I didn't send you to
the Holy Child to be serving coffee!

'I have been very close to Thea since she was born. I brought her on her first walk in a pram. Since she started school, I pick her up on a Friday and she comes to me. She is nine now. I am so proud of her. I have a room for her in my house, she picked out the wallpaper and everything.

'Kindness is the best value to pass on and I think I already pick that up in her as she is very kind and empathetic to people. She's very into her animals, which I think is a very nice trait. She has her own mind, which is why she is a woman after my own heart. She either likes something or she doesn't, and she is not going to wear something if she doesn't like it! She has been wearing horse-riding boots that do not fit her, but she likes them.

'I am not religious, but I believe in God. I would like her to believe in God. It doesn't mean that she has to go to church all the time, it doesn't have to be Jesus Christ, it could be Buddha, I don't mind. I would just like her to have something, a higher power to believe in.

'She likes flowers. I have always loved gardening, and I think liking nature and animals is important.

'I hope she has a happy life. I hope she finds her dream. She would like to work for the DSPCA, and she is adamant about that. I told her, "You have to study!" And she said, "I don't want to be a vet, I just want to look after the animals!" I don't necessarily want her to be academic, but I want her to reach her full potential. She is a great little reader, and she has an incredible imagination. I encourage her to do her art as well.

'I would like her to remember me with happiness, laughter, and that I made *amazing* pancakes. I would like her to remember me as warm and cuddly, and not just as her friend but someone she could come to if she had a problem.'

Grandchild age nine:
Thea

Acknowledgements

It was a privilege to write this book, to meet so many grandparents with so much in common. There was patience and kindness and lovely long chats about being a grandparent. We reminisced about our own childhoods and our grandchildren, swapped photos and shared our hopes for their futures.

But a book is all about teamwork, so I want to thank my husband, Brian, and my own children, Brian, Emily, Eoin, Maeve and Aengus, who were supportive and kind throughout the process. I can't leave the dogs out either, Ben and Sammy, who thought it was a bit strange for me to be reading aloud in the depths of night but who put up with it.

Thank you to all the wonderful grandparents who told me their stories and to Ruth McCormack, listener extraordinaire!

I mentioned teamwork and the team at Hachette who brought this book together are amazing. Thank you Ciara Considine, my editor, who constantly offered ideas and inspiration and who kept me on the straight and narrow. To Aonghus Meaney for his keen copy-editing, designer Karen Carty, cover artist Barbara Tibbets and all the team at Hachette Books Ireland.